ONE SURVIVOR'S GUIDE FOR BEATING

DEPRESSION AND THRIVING THEREAFTER

One Survivor's Guide for Beating Depression and Thriving Thereafter

*Simple, Practical, Step-by-Step
Remedies for the Illness of Depression*

by Nima Fard

The recommendations and suggestions in this book are a guide to be used in conjunction with medical supervision. Please ensure to consult your physician throughout.

Special thanks to Dr. Rajvir Dhillon for his eloquent contribution and Dr. Haydeh Esmaili for all of her help and guidance with this book.

This book is dedicated to my family.

Contents

Foreword

RAJVIR DHILLON, M.D.

What is becoming clear to many keen observers today is that humanity is no longer adequately meeting the demands of our increasingly complex, interconnected, uncertain and volatile world. Our current established approaches to many of our most pressing problems worldwide are insufficient and partially effective at best. In many areas of life, greater, broader, more diverse and integrated perspectives and approaches are required to meet this complexity, than what has heretofore been the norm. This intuitive push for a whole new way of seeing and doing things is very apparent in the field of healthcare of which I have been a part of for the last two decades as a physician in Canada. I say that much of it is intuitive because most people are unable to fully and consciously articulate what is exactly missing and yet they yearn for and are drawn in a certain direction – the direction of greater inclusiveness, and more perspectives being incorporated. In short, we want to embrace wholeness. Nima Fard's book, One Survivor's Guide for Beating Depression and Thriving Thereafter is a work that answers this call for those seeking a way through their depression.

There are numerous books out there on the subject of managing depression. What makes Fard's work refreshing is its treatment of the subject in a whole and complete fashion, incorporating physical, biological, social, emotional and spiritual approaches to it. The reader is exposed to up-to-date practical knowledge that speaks to all aspects of what makes us human in our struggle with depression. As a physician, I am all too well aware of the limitations of our modern, reductive approach to all aspects of medicine, but particularly in the area of mental health; our narrow clinical and biological means of relating to it, while ignoring the inner spiritual life, let alone emotional and social aspects of our being, is dehumanizing and costing us greatly as a society. It is well known, for example, that psychotherapy and medication are much more effective in the treatment of depression than

4

either approach alone. This fact alone already reveals how depression is much more than a "biological" disease. Despite this knowledge, we continue to struggle to provide patients with what should be the most rudimentary treatment. Most people only receive medications as treatment. When you consider numerous other aspects of depression as an illness, all touched on in this book, we could quite easily in a very cost-effective way manage depression more optimally and mitigate so much suffering as a society. This comes from simply seeing the disease from more angles, more perspectives than we currently do, nothing more. The parable of the three blind men and the elephant comes to mind. In contrast to the three blind men, Nima Fard's book is a view of your depression from 500 feet. You see it all, how it affects all aspects of your life, in its wholeness. He is a tour guide leading you through the terrain in a systematic fashion, so you see it in its entirety while managing all of it.

It is not just in the breadth of information he covers that the author brings wholeness. It is also in how he transmits it. As a practitioner of modern medicine, I have become increasingly dissatisfied with what I call the transactional

6

nature of the typical doctor-patient relationship. The doctor is less a true healer than a technician, an arbiter of specialized knowledge, whose purpose is only to deliver the appropriate knowledge and skills in a specified context. The interior dimensions of the healing relationship between the doctor and patient are often irrelevant. The source of all healing has been largely reduced to the medication. The doctor serves only as the medium. To state it in this manner is certainly a mild exaggeration, but the truth is that the consciousness of the physician, and as an extension, the healer-patient relationship, as an integral part of the healing process has increasingly become lost in our technologically driven medical system heavily influenced by the pharmaceutical industrial complex. In contrast, the compassionate voice of the author shines through the pages in this book. Amongst the factual information and advice, the author's personal story is interwoven throughout the book. He speaks openly of his healing journey, and in his exhortations, the reader can feel the presence of one who has emerged from the crucible to offer the reassuring and loving guidance from a higher place. Far from dispassionate, textbook information, the advice given in this book feels like it is coming from a supportive friend who has already taken the tumultuous journey and is reaching out his hand – one who is, at once, both an equal and a mentor. The book feels very personal and, yet, is a source of trusted health information. It is in this relational space where true healing transmission (not just the relaying of information) can occur.

I would like to conclude by highlighting what I believe to be the most significant contribution of this book. It is clear that the author understands that people in the throes of a deep depression need both a prescriptive step-by-step supportive guidance to an imagined finish line free from suffering, as well as the underlying wisdom that healing is a never ending soul journey in one's larger life narrative. This book implicitly recognizes this paradox of the healing process. That all disease leads to some form of suffering and that suffering is undesirable is axiomatic. However, in our instinctive need to avoid suffering, it is our nature to overlook its redemptive value. On a societal scale, this contributes to a medical culture that is consumed with alleviating symptoms and suffering at all costs while turning a blind eye to the greater transformative potential, both individual and collective, to which illness points. When we view illness as simply something that needs to be fixed and overcome, and not an integral part of our life's narrative journey towards becoming more whole, we miss out on a greater opportunity to discover who we are and experience a larger meaning in our lives. We unwittingly relegate that which needs to emerge from within us to the basement of our individual and collective psyche. Our desperate clinging to comfort and freedom from physical and psychological suffering cuts us off from the true fountain of youth – the greater life to which we are all being called. The secret that is whispered for the few willing to listen is that life was never intended for our comfort. Our symptoms are our soul's distant beacon that our ship is off-course. Don't ignore the signals, as Thomas Moore pleads in his seminal work Dark Nights of the Soul. Sit still and listen to what they are asking of us. This book contains the nurturing and supportive words to carry you out of the darkness of your depression while stressing the skills and practices that will allow you to actualize the potential that your illness is calling you to fulfill.

Rajvir Dhillon, MD

Doctor of Family Medicine, Calgary, AB.

Introduction

"…I am not afraid of storms, for I am learning how

to sail my ship."

-Louisa May Alcott

There is a very large gap in understanding when

it comes to the disease of depression. It is often

widely misunderstood by the friends and family of those who are going through it as well as the public at large. The fact that sufferers feel so alone and misunderstood as well as hopeless and frustrated requires a comprehensive solution, a guide that is not only steeped in helpful scientific information, but also empathy, guidance, and understanding. The reason I wrote One Survivor's Guide was to fill this gap; to shed light on the misunderstanding, and to raise awareness about the disease. It has been a long and emotional journey writing this book and I feel privileged to be able to share my story. If you are someone who is suffering from depression, I want to commend you for being brave enough to pick it up. I know how debilitating depression can be and how hard it is to take that all-important first step towards recovery. In this regard, you are one of the brave ones. I want you to know that this book has been written for you and that it will be addressed to you for its remainder. If you are someone who has a loved one living with depression and is not sure of what you can do, this book is also for you. Its narrative can help you to understand what those who are suffering are really going through, and its tools can guide you to help them heal. If you are someone who wants to live their best life and are looking to get out of a rut and start enjoying life again, then this book is for you as well. Its practices can center you and enable you to focus on the healthy lifestyle that you've always wanted. After all, we all need a push every now and then to help us be our best. The truth is that depression has many levels and degrees and can be everything from mildly annoying to utterly devastating. For the purposes of this book, I will assume that you are fighting through the worst kind. I know first-hand that if this is the case, then it can seem relentless and consuming.

The BBC recently reported that mental illness now affects 1 in 4 people, at one point or another, throughout their year ("Depression"). It seems that we all know someone who is suffering from depression and it is hard to truly know what they are really going through. Depression is also becoming more and more prevalent in our modern world as things become more complex and unstable. As we desperately search for quick solutions, we are often disappointed by their results. But there is hope. If you are one of those who are affected by the disease of depression, then I want you to know that, with some measure of consistent effort, it can be beaten. I want you to, truly, foster the hope of beating it in your mind. I also want to impart to you that your depression has, within it, the power to change your life for the better. Now, that concept may sound a bit crazy if you are currently within its suffocating grip, but my intention is, that as a result of the remedies and practices you will learn from reading this book, you will be able to win the battle and become much stronger than you ever were before.

I was once in an emotional place where I thought it was impossible to escape the illness of depression. I believed that I would never get better. In a way, I was trapped within the prison of my own mind. I was just waiting to get better and took no action. My fight with depression was hard, but somehow, after all of the struggle, I was able to survive. It all came down to one thing: Taking consistent action every day. That is all. When I started to take some action every day towards getting better, I began to slowly see positive results and the first glimmer of hope was born in my mind. The problem is that when you are depressed, it is very hard to take any action at all – you simply do not want to do anything. That is why I strongly believe that someone with depression, who is paralyzed by inaction, needs a coach, a friend, or an advocate – someone who will push them to take action. When I was in the worst of it, I didn't know where to start. I was lost in regard to what to do in order to feel better. I searched and searched, but was hard-pressed to find any useful information that actually worked. I examined and mined all of the information I could in an effort to find anything that could help. After years of research, I was eventually able to find the keys that worked for me. But it wasn't always simple. I learned that depression is a very complex disease, and getting better is just as complex. I knew that I would have to take an intricate mind-body approach to winning the battle. I knew that I would have to try and heal my mind, body, and soul – altogether. In the end, I found 17 successful remedies and actions that, when done together in a disciplined manner, helped me to ultimately win the battle. They are all outlined in this book for you. I am hoping that this book can be your coach, reference, and guide for winning the battle as well. My goal is that it will provide a holistic approach, and address the most important aspects of how you can heal your body and your mind.

The main purpose of this book is to share these

remedies as well as give hope to anyone who is at the end of their rope. To let them know that there is a way to get better, and that life can be enjoyable again. For those who are suffering, I have this message: You will be surprised at how strong you actually are! My promise to you is that you will be able to look back on your depression and see it for what it is: A life experience that taught you to persevere – one that helped you to grow into the person that you have always wanted to become. Unfortunately, if you're in the midst of your depression, then it is hard for you to feel this way. When you're under the distress of the disease, it is quite frankly hard to see anything as it truly is. Everything is skewed towards the negative. What I have learned is that you must question your negative thoughts and never believe them, when you are in a state of depression. Later on in the book, we will go over how to neutralize these types of negative thoughts by using mindfulness. You will learn these techniques and find that they are incredibly effective when you are under attack by your own thoughts. You will just need to practice them regularly.

Throughout this book, I will constantly be mentioning the little things that are important to do, in order to win the struggle. Tiny steps that on their own may seem small, but when combined all together, help to create synergistic habits that will allow you to gain momentum and win the ultimate battle. As you take these baby steps, you will start to see yourself in that place where you have control again – in that place where you can start to feel like yourself again. We will get there together.

For me, the worst part of my depression lasted three years and the whole of it lasted over five years. During those soul-grinding years, I came very close to giving up, but I was able to forge new habits that helped me to survive. In the upcoming chapters, I am going tell you bits of my story – small parts of how I felt and how I fought through it. I will also share the keys that helped me to win the battle.

Over the last ten years, I have read many books on the topics of depression, mental illness, Cognitive Behavioural Therapy, and the brain. I also read many books about diet, general health, meditation, mindfulness, and human development. Each book had a little bit of information that helped me. Many of these books shared a vast amount in common; they were each filled with important scientific research. They all contained some crucial information and wisdom that enabled me to begin my fight. I started to try the suggestions in these books, and to my surprise, they started to work wonders. The one thing I have learned from them is that the healing process is one that takes time. Patience and practice are needed to succeed. In many ways, I needed to test each piece of information for myself in order to see if it worked for me or not. My brain and body became a barometer – a testing ground for different foods, supplements, activities, and practices. The formula was very simple: If it made me feel better, then I continued to do it. If it didn't, then I stopped it. In every instance, when I was diligent and steadfast to sticking to the things that made me feel better, I began to see results. You too must start to listen very closely to your mind and body and see what practices help and what don't. Most importantly of all – you must try them out for yourself.

Now, let's get to the remedies. The upcoming chapters will be broken down into 17 crucial steps. The subjects range from diet and exercise, to practices like mindfulness and meditation, and even to topics such as sleep and breathing.

This book is the condensed culmination of years of trial and error, and its information can save you a lot of time. By themselves these steps are good, but when executed altogether they can be incredibly powerful. I wanted to include as much as I could without being too overwhelming. I, therefore, included only the most important and crucial information that I have learned throughout the years. For the most part, all it takes is doing them for at least a minimum of 30 days so that you can see if they really work for you or not. You will find that many of these suggestions just take persistence for them to be effective.

The upcoming steps are filled with a wealth of information that will help you to win your battle, but I do want you to know that there are no magic pills or fixes. Every remedy needs to be practiced and carried out in a disciplined manner. By continuously exercising your muscle of discipline, you can uncover the prospect of a new and healthy life – one that, with a little bit of hard work, can be realized. Throughout the book, I am going to ask you to push yourself outside of your comfort zone and open your mind to new possibilities. I am also going to ask you to follow through with all-important action.

I want you to scare yourself a little each day in regard to what you are capable of. With a small level of discipline and some determined action, great things can happen. The ripple effect of each small action will build on the last. It is gradual, and success is dependent on your ability to execute on a daily basis. Once these steps become new habits, then you will be able to accomplish positive changes that will stay with you for a lifetime.

Let's get started. The first four steps will take you to a place where you can start to regain control again. After that, the rest of the steps will fall into place. If these first four steps seem like they're overly simplistic, do not be discouraged. There is a method to it all. Each step is designed to compound on the previous step. In fact, this book is designed so that each step becomes more powerful when executed and practiced with the previous one. You will find that together, they will form the foundation of your recovery. In the end, they will help you to thrive.

Step 1 - Omega-3s

"If there is no struggle, there is no progress."

-Frederick Douglas

On my thirtieth birthday, I found myself in the hospital. I was there because of a mood disorder that I had inherited from my father. All throughout my life, I had witnessed my father spring in and out of mania and depression. When he was manic, he was filled with energy, passion, and at times, madness. When he was depressed, he barely spoke, and I could tell he was struggling to get through his days. He never complained, though. My father always displayed textbook, classic bipolar disorder. Up until my late twenties, I had thought that his illness had spared me but the preceding months to my own hospitalization, included me working two jobs at a frantic pace. This was my first experience with mania. I ended up in the hospital with symptoms of a nervous breakdown. My mania had interfered with my sleep, and my lack of sleep was causing irrational thoughts. As bad as that was, it was still not the worst. After I had been discharged, I fell into a depression that was nothing short of paralyzing. The best way I can describe it was that my brain had shut down completely. I rarely talked, I felt very slow; I felt no hope, and I felt like death would be a solution. The depression lasted close to five years in total, and it was the hardest thing I've ever had to go through. I was desperate to find an answer. Jobless and living at my parent's house, I began to go to the library every day in a desperate effort to research what, if anything, could help. What I found there would help me climb out of the black hole that I was in.

I had been suffering for months before I went to the library. Every morning I would wake up early beyond my control (early morning wakeups are in some people a symptom of major depression). It was as if I was forced to be awake and live through life instead of having the solace of sleep to escape to. When I started going to the library each day to pass the time and research depression, I was surprised at how little information there was on the subject. I searched and searched, but there was little in regard to how to treat the illness with natural remedies. One day, I got lucky and found a science-based book on a substance called eicosapentaenoic acid (EPA). EPA and docosahexaenoic acid (DHA) are the building blocks of omega-3 fatty acids. That book had the science I needed to begin taking my first step to recovery. It was the very first thing that helped me. It outlined the scientific evidence of how omega-3 oils, with high levels of EPA and DHA, can aid in fighting depression and help people suffering from the disease to feel better relatively soon. I immediately dropped the book, only having skimmed it for its crucial information, and frantically went to the drug store. There, I found omega-3 supplements. There were many different types with different concentrations of EPA and DHA. I found the brand with the highest concentration of both EPA and DHA and began taking a high dose.

After only two weeks of sticking to it, I felt like a miracle had happened. I felt my first sign of relief. I was still very sick, but I felt the first glimpse of light. The high dosage of omega-3s had made me feel about 20% better. I began to feel slivers of some emotion again. I began to feel partly human again. Nothing can explain the relief and gratefulness that I felt when I had discovered something that actually worked. My dosage was three 1000 mg gel capsules a day. Eventually, I started buying the liquid form of the oil and taking a teaspoon after each meal.

Let's talk about omega-3s. The reason omega-3s work so well and are so effective is that your brain is made up of fatty lipids. EPA and DHA play a very important role in the functioning of these lipids as well as overall brain function. One particular study mentions this by stating that, omega-3s are crucial components of the neuronal cell membrane, and that they benefit many mental disorders by regulating brain signalling as well as benefit the brain's neurotransmitters (Bozzatello et al.).

Thus omega-3s are necessary for both the makeup and structure of the brain as well as crucial for the proper functioning and release of neurotransmitters such as dopamine and serotonin. These findings, that support the idea that omega-3s are beneficial to maintain a healthy brain, are now widely accepted by the scientific community as facts. They are also great news for sufferers of depression. Another study concludes that the building blocks of omega-3s, which are DHA and EPA, reduce neuroinflammation as well as cognitive decline. They state that EPA affects mood, while DHA is essential to brain structure (Devassy et al.). As I will be mentioning over and over in this book, substances that reduce inflammation are key to beating depression and omega-3s are one of them.

This stuff works. It not only provided some relief to my major depression relatively quickly, but I continue to take it to this day to keep my brain in good health. I now take a lower daily dose, but I have found that it is still very effective in warding off the blues.

Now, there are many great ways to get omega-3s from food sources such as fish, nuts, and seeds, but if you are suffering I would suggest that you supplement with fish oil right away. The reason is that high-quality fish oil will give you the most potent dose of omega-3s and are more effective than any other source for fighting depression. Fish oil is also filtered and authenticated for purity and does not contain any of the mercury or heavy metals that fish or seafood may. The reason they are so effective is that purified fish oils have the highest concentration of EPA and DHA. If you are vegan or a vegetarian, you can eat foods that are high in alphalinolenic acid (ALA). ALA is converted into EPA and DHA once it's in your body. Some examples of these foods are walnuts, almonds, or pecans. Or seeds such as flaxseeds, chia seeds, or pumpkin seeds. You can also take concentrated oils that are high in ALA like flaxseed oil.

Now, getting your DHA and EPA from ALA conversion, as you do from these vegetarian options, will garner much less omega-3s in your body than a source that has EPA and DHA already in it – in this case, fish oil. Up to ten times less. And because you may be under the distress of the illness, and need something that will work relatively quickly, fish oils may be your best bet. Highly concentrated fish oils are even more potent in terms of EPA and DHA and could be the fastest way to get high amounts of EPA and DHA into your system at first. For me, what worked best for my depression was regular-concentration fish oil that was in liquid form; it offered the most efficient results in terms of real change in regard to my illness.

Taking all of this into consideration, if you

cannot take fish oil for any reason, it would be a good idea to increase your intake of omega-3s from food sources. My suggestion is that in order to most efficiently fight your depression, stick to foods with naturally high amounts of EPA and DHA already in them. Below is a list of foods that have these building blocks of omega-3s already in them.

Omega-3 Foods

- Fish – (most types of fish) Mackerel,

Salmon, Tuna, Sardines, Trout, Sea Bass, Pollock, Halibut, Herring, Whitefish, etc. (usually as a rule of thumb, the smaller the fish, the more omega-3s it contains).

- Seafood – (most types of seafood) Clams, Lobster, Mussels, Scallops, Oysters, Shrimp, Eel, Crab, etc.

- Sea vegetables – (most types of seaweed) Arame, Nori, Kombu, Wakame, Hijiki, Dulse, Agar, etc.

- Eggs – Fortified (or not) with omega-3s.

- Milk – Fortified with omega-3s.

Another great thing about omega-3s is that they

are beneficial for your heart health. One study, in the publication Atherosclerosis, states that heart patients that took omega-3 oils had, improved blood vessel function as well as improved arterial stiffness. They also say that omega-3s have an anti-inflammatory effect on the heart (Tousoulis, et al.). In fact, the anti-inflammatory effects of omega-3s have been shown over and over, in a wide variety of studies, to be not only good for the brain and the heart, but also good for the body. In this regard, omega-3s have been found to capably decrease inflammation of the joints in a number of studies. Most importantly, though, for our purposes, the majority of studies have shown the assured effects of omega-3s on the brain. One study even goes as far as to say that omega-3 oils increase gray matter volumes in the brain and thereby have positive effects on memory, affect, and mood (Conklin et al.).

In my case, it took a total of about six weeks to feel the full effects of the high dosage of omega-3s from fish oils. The gains felt like they were compounding. The more diligent I was about making sure to take them every day, the better the results. I did not overdo it. I stuck to the dose: one teaspoon of regular concentration fish oil after each meal – daily. I did not waver. One thing that you will see throughout this book is that once I found a key to unlock a secret to healing my depression, I continued to use it and was disciplined about doing it every day. You must understand that if you get complacent and stop doing the little things each day, you will stop seeing progress or not see it at all, to begin with. Just like a plant that does not get water and nutrition will wilt, wither, and die, your brain is very similar in regard to the nutrition that it needs. With omega-3s, my brain was beginning to receive the vital nutrition it needed to survive the ordeal of my illness and eventually start to heal. This was the beginning.

My suggestion in regard to your fight with depression is that you immediately start taking omega-3 fish oil. You can start off by taking the capsules which are easier than consuming the straight oil. Make sure to look for the ones with relatively high concentrations of EPA and DHA. This means that if you are taking a 1000 mg capsule, the percentage of EPA needs to be at least 40% and the percentage of DHA needs to be at least 30%. For example, that would be at least 400 mg of EPA and 300 mg of DHA in a 1000mg capsule. Start by taking one or two capsules with every meal. If you are of the brave, then go straight to taking the liquid oil by taking a teaspoon after each meal (max. 3 per day). You will find that after two weeks of taking omega-3s every day, you could start seeing the positive results. The only thing to be careful of is if you are taking blood thinner medication for your heart. If this is the case, then omega-3s may not be the best course of action as they may increase the risk of bleeding. Either way, make sure to consult your doctor with any new medications or supplements that you are taking on. In fact, throughout this book, I will be making suggestions for you and before you take action, make sure to let your doctor know.

Step 2 - Exercise

"There is no substitute for hard work."

-Thomas Edison

When I was at the worst stage of my depression, just the thought of exercise made me nauseous. I was at my worst when my friend came to visit me from Toronto. He is a well-respected doctor who specializes in internal medicine, so his arrival was not only a welcomed visit from a good friend but also a Godsend in terms of his knowledge and helpfulness about what I was going through. I was in such bad shape that in hindsight when I think back to that time, I realize that he was like an angel who was sent to help me. At that time, I had not yet discovered omega-3s and was in the midst of the worst part of my major depression. I could not think straight, and it was difficult for me just to be awake. I was in a constant state of discomfort and did not feel like doing anything let alone exercising. He saw how bad I was and I could

54

see the pain in his eyes. I could tell that it was hard for him to see his friend in pain. He reassured me that if I hung on things would get better. What he did next had such a profound effect on my day-to-day life, that I still do it to this day. He forced me to go for a walk every day. At the time, my appetite was so bad that I didn't want to eat anything. I would eat less than a quarter of a plate of food every night. I was very weak and fragile, and my body weight was down to 140 lbs. That was not a normal weight for me because when I was healthy, I was around 170 lbs. I remember I felt envious of his appetite. After dinner he would always say, "Okay man, let's go, let's go for a walk." I did not want to go at all. I remember that it was in the middle of summer and I kept beating myself up as I thought, "why can't I enjoy this good weather at all, why can't I enjoy anything?" Nevertheless, he persisted, and I conjured up all of the will I had, and we left the house together and started our walk. It was only about half a mile to the coffee shop that we had chosen as a destination, and I remember having to stop two or three times that first day because I began to dry-heave. It was a symptom of the anxiety that I was feeling all the time as well as the general anxiety I was feeling about the illness. I would stop and

56

begin retching, and he would say, "It's okay man, you're going get through this." The next day, needless to say, I did not want to go for the walk because I was afraid I was going to start gagging again. But he pushed me to go. This time, to my surprise, I didn't gag as much. We walked to the coffee shop and sat there for a few minutes and then walked back to the house. We did that for 5 or 6 days straight. Each day, I forced myself to do it. There were good walks and bad ones in between, but throughout his stay, I started to feel incrementally better. Those walks taught me that if you take some small action every day, it is better than not doing anything. I learned that just by doing something positive, like taking a walk every day, changes your intention and helps you to start to heal. I did not know it then, but I was beginning to start a wonderful new habit of moving when I felt bad. I must say that it was one of the most powerful habits I would ever learn.

Exercise is the key to well-being. Period. When you exercise, you are giving your body a cleanse. The oxygen that you are taking in is virtually giving life to and detoxing all of the cells in your body. The capillaries and blood vessels that deliver this oxygen everywhere in your body start to grow, develop, and expand throughout your body the more you exercise. This intricate network gets stronger and can deliver more and more oxygen to new places, and it also creates new healthy cells. Physical exercise will not only help you in regard to your depression, but it can help you with weight loss and to look younger; it can help you with your energy levels and your sleep; it can help you to consistently feel good. To form a habit of exercising every day is to form a habit that will not only vastly improve the quality of your life, it will start changing the fabric of who you are. It has always been my belief that exercise has a magical effect on not only improving your circulation but has a way of optimizing your genetics so that you are always growing and developing in a healthy way; especially as you age.

For someone who is ill, to start exercising is quite possibly one of the hardest actions to do. In many instances, depression manifests itself in negative ways in terms of one's energy levels, and people who are afflicted, constantly feel sluggish, tired, and sleepy. Sometimes they feel borderline catatonic. When I was at my worst, I could not run because I had no energy. Add to that the embarrassment I often felt when I ran in my neighbourhood because I would, again and again, dry-heave after a few minutes of jogging. I would usually cut it short and go back into the house feeling defeated. The key was, though, that I kept trying and fought through it. My suggestion to you is to start with simple brisk walks. I remember reading somewhere that brisk walks have a better effect on stress reduction than any other form of exercise. I have found this to be very true. Begin with walking. Walking and breathing. Very simple. If you already exercise regularly, then keep it up and push yourself a little harder if you need to. If not, then this next section is for you. Here is a simple suggestion on how to get started.

A Simple Start-to-Exercise Plan

1. Start out walking 10 minutes a day for 3 days. In those first 3 days, the most important thing is to show up and do it. Set a time that you will stick to, and simply just walk for 10 minutes. Do this for 3 days in a row.

2. After 3 days, increase it to 15 minutes a

day for 6 days. Now you are in the swing of it. Make sure you go at the same time every day and don't skip. Make it 15 minutes for 6 straight days. Take 1 day off for rest.

3. After one week, increase it to 20 minutes per day. Twenty minutes is your target to walk every day. Now that you have started to walk for 20 minutes a day, you are well on your way to developing a new healthy habit. If you can do those first 3 days for 10 minutes a day, then the others will fall into place. The key is to do it. Do

not talk yourself out of it. Don't think! Go

through with it.

4. There will be days when you are going to

get home from work and say, "Not today,

I'm too tired." Those are the days that

you must go. I promise you, if you go, 5

minutes into it, you will say to yourself,

"I'm glad I did it, I'm glad I went, " and

after you are done you will feel a strong

sense of accomplishment. More

importantly, you will feel a little bit better.

That's what will keep you coming back.

5. Set a time every day that you will take your walk and go no matter the weather, and no matter the circumstance. You may walk on a treadmill at the gym or at home. Just make sure that if you miss your time, you make it up later that day. Ensure that you go through with it. The key here is building the habit. Once you build the habit of going every day, it will eliminate the thought that is involved in it. That's what you want. You don't want a chance to think yourself out of it. You just want to go through with it – every day. Stick to it, and you won't regret it.

6. If you want to switch to running or jogging, then after you have walked for 1 whole month begin to swap the walking for jogging or running. Stick to the 20 minutes per day. Once you start jogging or running, then do 3 days on and 1 day off for rest. When you do this, you will be able to slowly build a foundation so that you can become a runner. How great will that be!

Exercise may initially have a small effect for some but, if done consistently, it will compound.

As you build a foundation of physical fitness, it has the capacity to heal you in a very powerful way. It is not something that will work right away like a magic pill. In fact, as we said before, there are no magic pills. You must learn to do the little things every day in conjunction with everything else. Exercise is one of those little things. Beating depression has a formula, and all of its little ingredients are important. That is how you will eventually beat it.

There have been innumerable studies done on the benefits of exercise, but one powerful paper sums them up well. In the article Exercise as medicine – evidence for prescribing exercise as therapy for 26 different chronic diseases, researchers found evidence that exercise is beneficial for the treatment and prevention of many different types of disease. They found that exercise helps to alleviate the negative symptoms of depression, anxiety, and stress, as well as battles diseases like diabetes and coronary heart disease (Pederson and Satlin).

My rule with exercise is that you must break a sweat. Even if you are walking, try and break even the smallest of sweats. When you do that, you know that you are making progress and getting somewhere. Continue to walk for 20 minutes a day for 1 month taking 1 day off a week for rest. After you have done it for a month, then you can start increasing your pace to a light jog and maybe even eventually run. Try to keep in mind that it doesn't have to be just walking or running; it can be any cardiovascular aerobic exercise. Try a stationary bike, or an exercise machine, or jumping jacks, or running on the spot. Just break a sweat for 20 minutes – at least 6 days a week. If you do that, then you will be starting a habit that will enrich your life for the better. The key is not to concentrate on what has happened leading up to now. If you were never able to exercise before, you must devise a plan on how to do it now. Be creative. It does not have to be conventional. Make sure not to tell yourself that you can't do it. We are all capable somehow. Remember, what happened in the past has nothing to do with how you create your future. Or better yet, how you create your present moment. As soon as you are doing it, you need to rejoice and celebrate it. Take in the feeling, and no matter how hard it may seem, I promise you, it will get easier the more you stick to it. You will need to build a foundation before you can truly start seeing the benefits. This all-important foundation begins with two things: A single step, and the persistence of showing up for yourself every day.

One of the most important aspects of cultivating and developing a habit that you will stick to is to ask yourself, "How can I do this and have fun doing it?" On many nights I would come home from work and think, "I'm too tired today," and would talk myself out of going. What I found out was that if I ended up going, 5 minutes into it, I was happy that I pushed myself to go. Even more powerful was how I felt afterward. Because of that feeling, I learned that if I ever started to talk myself out of it, I would not listen and just stick to the original plan of going.

People used to ask me why I run and I use to say so that I could prove to myself that I am worth a damn. Now when they ask me, I tell them it is the key to my well-being. When you exercise, your hormones become balanced and regulated naturally. You start seeing things from a perspective of I can do it, and it all happens because of the hormones that are activated as a result of the exercise. It's a wonderful cycle. Along with this, you get the added benefit of the natural release of endorphins and anti-depressant neurotransmitters in your brain as well. It all comes with a bit of work and some persistence. Remember, once you decide that you are going to act, then you are already empowered. Start today.

As you start your walks, I want you to begin to notice the benefits of breathing. One thing you will need to remember is that your breath is everything. Oxygen is quite possibly the best thing on earth! It is everywhere, and it's free. I'm very excited to share with you the next step; it is all about the miracle of breath.

Step 3 - Diaphragmatic Breathing

"I meet my Self in stillness, and we breathe."

-S.W. Berry

You may be thinking that breathing is not all that

important of a topic when it comes to

depression, but as we cover meditation and mindfulness practices, later on, you will see that learning how to breathe correctly is the foundation of many of the practices in this book. It is a vital key to your future success. For me, learning how to breathe correctly was a turning point to being able to exercise better, discover stress relief, have more energy and achieve peace in my day.

As I started to feel a little bit better each day with the addition of omega-3s and exercise, I was seeking a way in order to quell my anxiety. At the time, I felt immense stress about the depression, and it had a terrible effect on me. I kept thinking, "How did I get here?" "How did it get so bad?" I had lost faith in myself, my abilities, and my future. I just didn't think that I would ever be able to get back to the person I used to be: That capable, high functioning person that graduated university and worked downtown at the big financial firms. I needed a way to calm my thoughts and reduce my stress. I was still in the grip of the disease, and I had to start to push myself to maybe start something new and maybe get a job again. Just the thought of being back in the workplace terrified me. In the past, I was successfully working in the financial industry for various financial companies, but at that time the idea of going back in that lion's den of pressure seemed impossible. I just didn't have any belief in my abilities; I had no confidence that I'd be able to handle real responsibilities again. I needed something that would calm my nerves when I was wound up – something that could help me to start again. That's when I discovered diaphragmatic breathing as a tool for alleviating the negative symptoms of stress and helping with my depression. It worked well as a relaxation tool and would ultimately help me to summon up the courage to think about beginning again. I started to learn how to breathe diaphragmatically. For me, it was the start of a great relationship with breathing. What I eventually learned was that deep, diaphragmatic breathing is the foundation of many forms of stress management and the integral base of helpful practices like meditation and mindfulness. I started to use it to get myself strong again – to try again.

As babies, we start out breathing with our whole bodies. When you watch a baby breathe, its stomach moves up and down, in and out, filling and emptying to its full capacity. Babies naturally breathe like this, and it aids them in their growth and rapid development. When we reach adulthood, we cease to breathe like this. Our breath becomes shallow and quick. In fact, any time we take long, deep breaths we are amazed at how effective they are in helping us to feel relaxed and calm. Long, deep breaths should be used all the time, not just when we are feeling stressed. The way to do this is to learn the art of diaphragmatic breathing.

Diaphragmatic breathing uses the entire cavity of your torso, diaphragm, and stomach in order to fill your lungs with air and optimize the amount of oxygen that you receive. It cannot only help you to relax; it can help you to have more energy. It can help you to get through long hours at work and give you that extra push that may be needed to get through the day. I have always thought that people who smoke do it because it is an opportunity to go outside, have some alone time, and take long deep breaths. Yes, they are inhaling smoke, but the fundamentals are similar to deep breathing in many ways. They are taking a break and giving themselves a moment outside. Those smoke breaks can often be a time of quiet contemplation and peace. With diaphragmatic breathing, the concept is the same, but it is not harmful in any way. In fact, it is probably one of the most powerfully healthy things you can do throughout the day to feel better. The best part is that it is very simple to learn, and it's totally free. The hard part is to remember to do it daily. If you add it to your daily regime, it will transform the quality of your life. First, set a time to do it for 5 minutes every day. Once you have done it for one month, you will use it again and again. So how do you do it? Well, it is relatively easy, and once you get the hang of it, you'll be utilizing it all the time.

As with anything else, diaphragmatic or belly breathing gets better with practice.

Diaphragmatic Breathing Made Easy

Start out by lying on the floor on your back in a comfortable position. Put one hand on your belly. Now, as you inhale, push your belly out so that the air can fill your belly. As you exhale, suck your belly in. As you do this, the hand on your belly can guide your breathing, always being there, to measure your breath. Make sure to push your belly out all the way, when you inhale. This may feel strange at first, but once you get the hang of it, it will be your go-to method of breathing when you are out of energy or need to relax. When you exhale, make sure you do it fully as well, sucking your belly in, so that all of the air goes out. Begin by inhaling to a slow count of 7, and also time your exhale to a slow count of 7. Always remembering to physically push your belly out when you are breathing in and pull it all the way in when your breathing out. Do this for 10 repetitions each session. Do this session throughout the day

84

when you need it.

This method will give you much more oxygen than your regular shallow breathing. I always found that when I was stressed, I would do some diaphragmatic breathing and almost every time I would find another gear to tackle the problem. Adopting a breathing practice is not only good for stress relief, but it is also a way to invigorate and has been shown to improve cognition. One study, that supports the science behind the beneficial effects of taking on a breathing practice, was conducted by researchers, Soni, Joshi, and Datta. What they found was, that after six weeks of controlled deep breathing practice, individuals' cognitive abilities improved (41).

Diaphragmatic breathing is the type of breathing we will explore and develop throughout this book. As we cover meditation and mindfulness practices in the upcoming chapters, I encourage you to use diaphragmatic breathing as the main method of breathing for them as well. I now diaphragmatically breathe when I'm practicing meditation, mindfulness, and also do it when I'm exercising. Once you have the general mechanics down, you will only need to set aside around 5 minutes at different times throughout the day to practice it. As you do it more and more, you will find that you will want to do it all the time.

Like I said before, count to 7 as you breathe in and to 7 as you breathe out. Do this very slowly for 10 repetitions as you push your stomach out when you inhale and pull it all the way back in when you exhale. Afterward, you will feel better whether it be invigoration or relaxation. If you still require clarification, then there is an application that you can get for your iPhone or Android device called Breathe2Relax. It has a video showing you how to diaphragmatically breathe. It also has guided sessions that can help you to do breathing exercises along with music and pictures. I encourage you to download this app and try it out. I found the instructional video at the beginning very helpful and noticed that it helped me to master diaphragmatic breathing very quickly.

As I began to breathe diaphragmatically each day, I felt that with each breath, I was slowly becoming stronger. I began to visualize myself getting back into the workforce. Even though my mind was still filled with negative thoughts of everything that could go wrong, I felt like I was at a stage where I could start again. I began applying for jobs, and I eventually landed one at an insurance brokerage. I cannot stress the importance of pushing yourself outside your comfort zone when you are in the midst of your depression. When you are ill, your mind will always give you reasons not to try, reasons to stay in your comfort zone, and reasons why it won't work. You must learn not to listen to that voice and move forward. Later on in the book, we will go over methods that can help with this. Remember, do not listen to the voices that try to convince you that you cannot do it. For me, when I started that first job during my depression, I was very tentative and very quiet and unlike my normal self. I genuinely believed that I was going to fail. I had to push myself to get out of bed. I took things one day at a time and made sure that each day I built on the progress of the day before. That first job back required that I study for an exam for insurance brokers. Just the thought of an exam terrified me. I kept thinking over and over that I would fail. There was a delusion that I was convinced of at the time: that my brain was too damaged to be able to learn new concepts. Needless to say, when I was depressed, my mind would come up with all sorts of imaginative reasons of how I would fail. In fact, all brains do this. You need to question it when it does. I studied for the exam for two months. I'd go to the same coffee shop every night after work and go over the concepts, but they just felt like they weren't going into my head. I often called my best friend and would relay to him that I was sure to fail. On the morning of the exam, I was very nervous and began to dry heave – that old, familiar response to fear. I finally resolved to go into the exam room and give it my all. I was exhausted, but I took my time and breathed through it. My mark came back, and I had not only passed it, but I got

89%. I was so shocked and surprised that I didn't fail! It was incomprehensible. How did I do it? It showed me that, at that stage of my depression, everything that I thought about the world was negative, including the beliefs that I had about my own abilities. I learned right then and there that what my mind was telling me was not the truth. Not in the state that I was in. The fact was that I had pushed myself and succeeded, even when my negative beliefs were strong, and it made me feel like I had turned a corner in my recovery. The breathing definitely helped me to get there. It calmed me and helped me to push through. I began to look for more ways to calm my mind so that I could keep moving forward,

and that's when I discovered meditation.

Step 4 – Meditation

"Quiet the mind and the soul will speak."

-Ma Jaya Sati Bhagavati

Meditation is an ancient practice that I stumbled upon by accident, and I was lucky to do so. It has, over the years, had an exceptionally beneficial effect in regard to healing my depression as well as keeping my mind sharp. As I started breathing diaphragmatically, I noticed the positive benefits and thought to myself, "How can I go further?" "How can I use this breathing to heal my brain?" At the time, I was having trouble expressing myself. I wouldn't talk much, if at all. I still was only a shell of who I used to be before my depression. This was evident mainly regarding my personality and the effect that I had on others. Some close friends even mentioned to me that I was not the same person. Not as engaged. I needed something that would accelerate my healing – something that would heal my brain. I, therefore, endeavoured to meditate. I started reading book after book on meditation and began to research the topic online. As I practiced more and more, I started to slowly become comfortable with it and soon discovered that it was helping. I eventually found a simple method to meditate that really worked for me. I noticed that much of the literature that I read on the subject, contained within them, a lot of spiritual connotations that did not fit in with my particular spirituality. I, therefore, began to seek out simpler forms of meditation, and I started to distil my own elegant method from all the books I read.

I eventually personalized, formed, and developed a method that works well for me. Hopefully, it will work well for you as well. This method was integral to my healing and gave me the opportunity each day to feel better – even if it was momentary and in small increments. Those increments eventually added up over time, as I stuck to it, and solidified meditation as an important part of my daily routine. I began to meditate twice a day and it not only centered and healed me, but it allowed me to start enjoying life again.

Let's go over the basics of what this simple practice entails and the easy steps that can help you to start meditating. The following paragraphs will outline what is necessary for you start your own successful meditation practice even if you are very new to it and are unsure of whether or not you can do it.

If you think about it, your brain never rests. It is on all day, every day. When you are awake, when you sleep and even when you dream. Your brain needs moments when it can rest. Meditation is that rest. Not only is meditation good for healing depression, but it is also beneficial for improving focus, creating calm, and spurring creativity. Once you start to practice it, you will notice its benefits within a few weeks. The problem with meditation is that nobody thinks they're doing it right. The fact of the matter is that nobody does it perfectly and there is no perfect way to do it. The point of meditation is not to be in a state of absolute bliss and nirvana as you meditate. The point is to direct your mind to focus on what you want it to focus on. By doing this, you are creating tiny spaces where your brain can rest. Meditation is very simple: all you are doing is consciously attuning your attention to your breath. That's it.

100

If you ask many of the wisest, most enlightened gurus they will tell you, "The breath, always back down to the breath." When you constantly keep taking your attention back to your breath, you will find that there will be moments when you are able to fall into meditation and let your mind rest. That's it. Emptying your mind of thought and focusing on your breath. It's as simple as that. As thoughts come into your mind, you just release them into the blackness of your closed eyes. As more thoughts keep coming (and they will) you just keep releasing them and focus your attention back to your breath – over and over. As you keep doing this, you will find that there will be brief moments of thoughtlessness within your mind. This thoughtlessness is meditation. This is when your mind gets the rest that it needs and is in a meditative state. Some call this falling into the gap – that momentary period of silence and peace in your mind.

There is a reason why many people don't stick to meditation. They tend to think that because they have constant thoughts throughout their experience, it's because they are doing it all wrong. Let me tell you that I have been meditating for years, and I still have thoughts when I meditate. It is, in fact, a big part of the process. I nevertheless, still reap the benefits of meditation because when I do reach those brief states of thoughtlessness, I feel their positive effects. Those moments of thoughtlessness take me into a deep, trance-like state that heals and rests my brain. When I started to meditate regularly, in the midst of my depression, it helped me to focus my attention, even for minutes a day, on something other than the negative thoughts of my illness. This reason alone was worth doing it every day. As I got better, the reasons why I meditated changed. I now do it in order to spur creativity and hone focus. I have even, at times, reached that level of pure bliss while meditating that I thought was unattainable when I first started. The point is that I kept at it and I got better. You too can definitely get there too. However, you need to practice it daily and go through the ups and downs of it. You must make it into a process of discovery. That is why it is called a practice – it needs to be done daily in order for it to be effective and for it to reveal itself to you. Once again, if there is any suggestion I can give to you, it is that if you start something new and you perceive it to be good – then keep at it – you will eventually reap the rewards.

Meditation How-To

Now, let's talk about how to meditate. A simple rule of thumb is to start small. You do not need to meditate for more than 5 minutes at a time when you first start out. As you get better at it, you can extend the time. If you think about it, in the course of the day, 5 minutes is a very short time. Remember that, that short amount of time is giving your brain an invaluable rest.

Start with finding a place that is quiet where you won't be disturbed for at least 5 minutes. You may sit either on the floor, in a comfortable position, or on a chair with good posture. Posture is important because as you sit up, you automatically become consciously aware of your body. Body awareness has very much to do with noticing yourself and your surroundings. This is important as you meditate because it helps to bring you into the moment. Posture also helps in making sure that you don't fall asleep as you meditate. As a result of your posture being upright and engaged, you can stay alert and awake.

As you sit, start with a few deep breaths. As you exhale, begin to focus all of your attention to the air going in and out of your belly. You can also focus on the air going in and out of your nostrils. Feel your breath going in and out in a diaphragmatic way. As you practice diaphragmatic breathing more and more, this will become quite easy and comfortable to do.

Now, as you breathe in and out, focus on your breath and consciously clear your mind of all thoughts. As you do this, you will for moments feel yourself going into brief periods of a trance-like state. This will naturally happen, as you continuously focus on your breath and consciously empty your mind of thoughts. Let it happen smoothly and naturally. This is the process of letting go. This is the process of falling into the gap. This is the process of allowing yourself to drift into a deep meditative state.

When thoughts come into your mind, and thoughts will keep coming: about work, or loved ones, or anything at all, just direct your mind back down to your breath and let the thoughts clear away. Think of them dissolving, like powder into a vast blue ocean. As you do this, let your mind naturally expand, and keep focusing back down to your breath. You will get better and better at directing your attention to your breath as you keep doing this.

When thoughts come up, once again, consciously clear them away. See those thoughts dissolve one by one, into an enormous blue ocean.

As you seamlessly focus back on your breath, you will once again fall momentarily into a helpful and restful trance. This is what meditation is – the constant refocusing and redirection of your mind. This is what heals you.

This is what gives your mind rest.

You may hear noises around you as you meditate. Do not worry about these noises distracting you as they can help you go deeper into a state of trance. Simply just notice them getting either louder or quieter and fall into them as well. That's all.

As you go deeper and deeper into meditation, make sure to keep focusing your attention back down to your breath.

You may set a timer for however long you want to do it. I would suggest that in the beginning, you do it for 5 minutes or so.

If you thought that meditation was more complicated than that, then I'm sorry to disappoint you. It is just about constantly focusing on your breath and letting your thoughts dissolve away. Once you do that, then you can naturally allow the healing trance to take over for brief moments. It is essential to be powerful in practice. This is meditation.

Meditation is a perfect time to practice your

diaphragmatic breathing, and you will notice that just by breathing deeply for a period of time you will be cleansing your body and blood with oxygen as well as coming back to the world refreshed and refocused. Pretty simple right? Just make sure that if you have sessions that are constantly filled with lots of thoughts, not to beat yourself up. It's natural. Just make sure your intention is focused on getting to those trance-like states for brief moments as you focus on nothing else but your breathing. Keep emptying your thoughts as your breath goes in and out, and you will feel the cleansing nature of the air. You will then start to feel the relaxed and engaged nature of your posture, and the next thing you know you will fall easily into those trance-like states. When you do reach those states of trance, you will start to begin to heal and grow your brain. These trance-like moments don't last long, but they are crucial in regard to your brain getting the rest that it needs. These states are much like the feeling of your eyes rolling deep into the back of your head when you are sleeping. The trance naturally occurs when you focus on your breath and dissolve your thoughts. If it helps, let your eyes roll back naturally as you fall into these trances. This is falling into the gap.

Studies have shown that after meditating for up to six months, individual's brains actually get bigger in size. One revealing study published in a popular psychiatry journal mentioned that those with chronic pain who had anxiety and depression may be able to find relief from a meditation practice. This supports the fact that meditation is not only good for depression but also beneficial in relieving anxiety (Rod and Kim).

You absolutely can begin to meditate. Set aside some time every day. A few minutes is nothing, and the benefits are immense. I did it every day for three months and found that my memory, focus, attention, creativity, sleep, and mental agility all were improved. My suggestion is that you meditate right before lunch and dinner every day. Once you get the hang of it, you can even start doing it two or three times a day. Always start with around 5 minutes. Eventually you can work up to longer periods. There is an old zen saying, "You should sit in meditation for twenty minutes a day unless you're too busy then you should sit for an hour."

I always found that after I had meditated, I was

able to tackle another set of problems. As my days got more hectic and I got tired, I would meditate, and it would be like recharging my mental battery. In a lot of ways meditation recharges and invigorates when you need it to and relaxes and rejuvenates when you need it to. Your brain will use it accordingly to balance itself out naturally. Just don't forget: if you are focusing on your breath, then you are doing it right. There are no bad sessions. Every time you sit with the intention to rest your brain and meditate, then you are healing it, developing it, and growing it. Always remember that.

Out of the all of the suggestions so far, meditation is one of the harder practices to continue to do every day on a consistent basis. The reason is that most people just don't make enough time for it. In my case, just taking those few breaks during the day, in order to have quiet moments, was great. Those moments of thoughtlessness always helped me to re-center, and I always came out of it feeling a little bit better. If you too begin to take some time for yourself and practice meditation, you may find that it can help immensely. I encourage you to start the practice. Set reminders on your phone, put notes on the fridge, or just simply step away for a few minutes to a quiet place. Begin your meditation practice, and it will not only accelerate your healing – it will improve the quality of your life. I promise.

After a few months of meditation, I found that my ability to sleep improved. I felt myself seeing the combined benefits of the omega-3s, exercise, and diaphragmatic breathing. I was gaining momentum, and my depression symptoms began to improve. Over the course of 8 or 9 months of doing the little things every day, I began to become more and more disciplined in my routines. I went for my walks every day, and they eventually turned into jogs. Those jogs eventually became runs. I slowly began to build on the successes of the day before. I began incorporating diaphragmatic breathing into my exercise and pre-sleep routine as well as my daily meditation practice. All of these things began to heal me slowly. I was on the right track.

I soon found out, though, that I could not get to the next stage of my healing until I began to seriously re-evaluate my diet. I often found myself very sleepy at work after meals. Something was still making me feel groggy and foggy all the time. I discovered that my diet was hurting me, and I endeavoured to change it.

Step 5 - Diet

"Let food be thy medicine and medicine be thy food.

"

-Hippocrates

You may have heard the expression that food is

either poison or medicine. I believe that this

statement is true for those who suffer from

depression as well as every living person. The diet and supplements step is the longest and most detailed step in this book, and there is a very good reason why: one of the most powerful ways to change how you're feeling, at any given moment, is by changing what you put into your body. An incredibly important lesson that the struggle with depression has taught me is that my diet directly correlates with how I feel throughout my day and on a day-to-day basis. Now, as you probably know, there have been countless books written on countless types of diets, and they are all filled with scientific information which is at times conflicting and at times quite overwhelming. I can tell you that when I started reading all of these books, I did not know which ones to follow. There was so much divergent information that it was hard to choose a course of action. I, therefore, tried them all. I tested everything out on myself and closely monitored what helped and what hurt. As a result, I was able to distil all of that information into 11 Diet Rules that I now live by. In terms of the books and articles that I read, I started to see some very important commonalities. Those books and their science helped me to determine which types of foods I needed to consume and how I needed to consume them in order to beat depression. In relation to the scope of this book, the suggestions that I have made in terms of diet, and the information that I have chosen to share, are based on the research that I have done as well as the results that I have experienced. These 11 Diet Rules are based on information that is commonly found in books and articles that reference how to fight depression as well as how to foster a healthy and balanced diet. They have been integral to my struggle, and they work! I have had the opportunity to test these broad rules out for over ten years, and I believe that they may be the best way for you to begin to change your diet for the better. The great thing about them is that they are not too complex or restrictive, so you are free to design your own food choices based on your specific tastes and personal preference. These rules will not only help guide you to develop healthier diet habits that will make you feel better in the midst of your illness, but they will give you the tools for mapping out your own diet plan that will lead to more energy and more vitality.

This chapter also contains information on a few powerful supplements that have helped me in my fight against depression. Like the 11 Diet Rules, these too have been tested by me and can help you get on the road to feeling better and staying better.

Before we explore the diet rules, I want to mention that the suggestions in this chapter are hard to live up to because of the stronghold that unhealthy food has in our lives. These foods are often romanticized and affectionately called "comfort food," thereby making them even harder to give up. In this regard, I want you to know that if you are diligent in taking on even some of these suggestions, you can not only feel better every day, you can actually achieve your ideal weight, reduce your body fat, and even attain the body that you have always wanted. You will realize, as you continue to read the chapters of this book, that everything is interrelated. The ideal self that you can become is a direct result of taking action and seeing the compounding effects of each and every one of these steps. The information contained in the 11 Diet Rules, that I'm about to share, is purposely meant to be simple and not too overly wrought with complex instructions. The reason for this is that too much information in terms of diet can be counter-productive, and as a result, one never knows which actions to take. You will find that with these elegant diet rules and a few adjustments, you can take your body, brain, and overall health to a new level where you can find your ultimate well-being. Most importantly, you will immediately find that these rules will have a positive effect on your mood and help you to effectively fight your depression. Let's get right into it!

11 Diet Rules

Diet Rule Number 1: Eventually

eliminate these types of foods from your diet:

The Deadly Five

- Artificially Processed Food

- Simple and Refined Carbohydrates

- Hydrogenated Fats (Trans Fats)

- Deep Fried Foods

- High Sugar Foods

If you eat these types of food, then you are not helping yourself to feel good in the four to five hours after consuming them. The Deadly Five can make you feel groggy, sleepy, and foggy. From my experience, they are also very addictive. An example of the negative effect that these types of foods have on someone, even those who do not suffer from depression, is that they feel like sleeping after eating them. Sleepiness after a meal is usually caused by the following: either eating too much food, or eating food that is high in fat, sugar, carbohydrates, and is artificially processed. These foods may taste very good when initially consumed but are detrimental for your body and brain. They are also extremely habit forming. A recent study found that highly processed foods that are rich in fat and high in refined carbs are in fact extremely addictive therefore making them drug-like and very hard to stop eating. A great article on the addictive quality of these types of foods concluded that: highly processed foods are like narcotics, in that they have a rapid rate of absorption into the blood and are often taken in high doses. They, therefore, are to blame for the tenacity of food addiction (Schute et al.).

These types of food are, I dare say, dangerous. They alter the way we feel very quickly and affect our brains negatively, in that, they either make us feel sleepy and groggy or take us on a short-lived fat and sugar high that has a sharp crash thereafter. The goal needs to be to start to wean these types of food slowly and gradually out of your diet. The way to do this is to begin to start eating them in very small amounts. These types of foods can be very difficult to quit cold turkey when you first want to make a change. You will need to start gradually decreasing the amounts of them that you eat in order to start to gain some control. We will soon discuss how to do this with portion control, but for the time being, understand that The Deadly Five have the power to affect your mood in a negative way.

One of the things I would like you to start doing is to do your own research, to a certain extent, so that you can see first-hand the overwhelming evidence and medical opinions that are associated with the dangers of these foods. For example, hydrogenated fats or trans fats have been proven by countless studies to be very bad for your heart health. Trans fats are found in pre-made cakes and cookies, crackers, vegetable shortening, margarine, chips, and doughnuts just to name a few. These foods are not only bad for your heart – they are bad for your brain. In one very revealing study, researchers tested the effects of these types of foods on mood and concluded that the lower the intake of trans fats, the better the mood. While also, the higher the intake of trans fats, the worse the mood (Ford et al.). If you want to maintain a positive mood, try to stay away from food that contains these dangerous types of fats. Deep fried foods are no better. They have also been shown in countless studies to be the cause of dangerous diseases. Like mentioned before, the amount of these foods that you eat is very important and crucial to determining whether or not they can make you sick. One brilliant study performed a comprehensive review of multiple different studies, in regard to the negative effects of fried foods, and examined the evidence as a whole. They concluded that chronic disease (all types) are linked to the consumption of fried foods (Gadiraju et al.). The fact that fried foods are known to cause chronic diseases should be enough reason for you to stay away.

Processed foods are part of The Deadly Five for a very important reason: they can be detrimental to your cognitive abilities. One study revealed that processed meats were in this category. They gave children different types of food and then tested their cognitive abilities. In their study, these researchers found that the more healthy foods you eat, (fruits, vegetables, whole grains, fish) the better and more positive the cognitive functioning of your brain. Conversely, they found that the less healthy you eat, (sugary foods, unhealthy snack foods, red and processed meats) the more negative the cognitive functioning of your brain. Through their research, they were able to suggest a positive link between healthy foods and brain performance (Cohen et al). These findings sum up the thesis of this diet step well in that they prove that the functioning of the brain is directly related to the types of food that you consume. Now, we will get to which types of food are good in the upcoming diet rules but for now, understand that if you are avoiding the bad and consuming the good, you are taking a step in the right direction when it comes to your brain health.

The next culprit on The Deadly Five list is the consumption of high amounts of simple carbohydrates. Consuming carbs in large quantities is oftentimes just as bad as eating sugary foods. This is because your body turns simple carbs into fat very quickly. Consuming high amounts of simple carbohydrates also leads to a high-glycemic-load and this, in turn, can affect mood and energy levels in a negative way. One study revealed this by stating that foods that contribute to a high-glycemic load contribute to depression, fatigue, and bad moods, whereas those with a low-glycemic load do not (Breymeyer et al.). In fact, it is widely accepted that consumption of too many simple carbohydrates, is detrimental to mood. This effect of high-glycemic load that simple carbs create in your system is even more prevalent when you eat foods that are high in sugar. In fact, sugar is so deadly that I gave it its own diet rule. It's coming up soon. For now, just remember to regulate and monitor your intake of simple carbs in order to ensure that your moods are not negatively affected.

If you become more cognizant of The Deadly Five and start to regulate how much of them you consume, you will be on the right path to better health and better moods. Begin to examine the foods types of food you eat and see if they fall into the category of The Deadly Five. If you do this, you can start to take the first steps to slowly decrease your intake of these bad foods and eventually eliminate them from your diet completely. Be diligent. It will take some self-control and discipline at first, but once you gradually start to cut them out, you will see how great you will feel as a result. The key is to replace the bad with the good. So, what is the good stuff you ask? It is in the next rule, and you can say that it's not only good, it's magnificent!

Diet Rule Number 2: Increase these types of food in your diet:

The Magnificent Seven

- Fruits

- Vegetables

- Whole Grains

- Fish, Seafood, and Lean Meats

- Beans

- Seeds and Nuts

- Fiber-Rich Foods

Unlike the foods to avoid, if you mainly eat the foods in the above list like fruits, vegetables, fish, seafood, lean meats, beans, and nuts you will not only feel lighter on your feet, but your brain will benefit as a result. The biggest advantage of eating healthy foods like these is that you won't feel foggy, sluggish, or sleepy after you eat them. You will also, as a result, have much more natural energy and feel great after consuming them. Other positive by-products of including these types of food in your diet are elevated mood, enhanced creativity, and reduced stress levels. These types of foods need to become your go-to when it comes to designing your meals. They are the key to choosing a healthy alternative. Now, there have been many books written on the health benefits of these foods and countless studies on how they help the disease of depression. One particular study titled, Food patterns and the prevention of depression, outlines the exact types of foods to eat. They conclude that foods that reduce the risk of depression are foods like vegetables, fruits, nuts, and seafood (Martinez-Gonzalez et al.). When faced with The Deadly Five, you should always turn to The Magnificent Seven as an alternative. Do this swap enough times, and you will build a habit that will improve your life. It will not only help you to beat depression, but it will help you to thrive on a consistent basis. For now, begin to start to classify food in your mind and either label them as part of The Deadly Five or The Magnificent Seven. Once you start to do this on a regular basis, you can begin to be more discerning in regard to what you eat. Every time you make a healthy choice, you will feel the difference that it makes on your mental state and mood. This will eventually help you to consistently make better choices going forward. If this all seems too good to be true, I promise you it's not. Some of the biggest keys to well-being in this book are incredibly simple. It's just a matter of execution. Now, some of the foods on The Magnificent Seven list have their own diet rules coming up, but for now, know that if you increase your intake of fruits, vegetables, nuts, beans, seafood, lean meats, and fiber-rich foods, you can begin to improve your diet for the better.

Diet Rule Number 3: Portion control

Portion control is in many ways the key to cutting out the bad foods in your diet. I was able to begin to slowly and drastically reduce the fatty, processed, carb-laden, and sugary foods from my daily diet just by reducing their portions in my diet. I found that in the beginning when I tried to stop eating foods that were from The Deadly Five list, I just couldn't do it. The more I tried not to eat them, the harder it was for me. What I discovered was that in terms of The Deadly Five, I just needed to reduce their portions gradually. For example, instead of eating two bowls of ice cream I would only have one scoop instead and then practice some self-control. I made it a game. This showed me that I could still have the foods that I craved in strict moderation. I also learned that if I regulated their amounts consistently, they would not have a negative effect on my mood. This concept of portion control helped me to regulate the amount I ate during meals as well. I rarely over-ate as a result. In time, I eventually weaned myself completely off of the fatty, processed, sugary, and carb heavy types of food altogether by using portion control. I was successful because I did not take a black and white approach to it. I did it slowly by gradually reducing the portions I had. I soon found out that portion size was the magic key to feeling good in regard to my brain and weight management in regard to my body.

I began to apply this principle to my meals and would always try to eat until I was only 3/4ths full. This is very important. My advice to you is to never eat until you are completely full or worse still – over-eat. What you'll learn by doing this is that, if you eat until you are 3/4ths full and wait five to ten minutes after you have finished your meal, you will not feel hungry anymore and will consequently not over-eat. You will also feel lighter on your feet and mentally sharper as a result. The reason for this is that it generally takes some time for food to digest and raise your blood sugar so that your body can tell your brain that you have reached fullness. We typically continue to eat after we are full because the glycemic feedback loop is delayed and we feel like we are not full yet as we eat – so we keep eating. You must take control of this. Eat to 3/4ths full, and then stop. Wait 5 minutes, and then you will not be hungry anymore. This method takes practice and a bit of self-control at first but if you do this regularly, you will be starting a new habit of portion control that will ensure that you never again feel groggy again after a meal. Over time, you will even find that your stomach will actually shrink and you'll require smaller portions in order to feel full. This will not only help with your mood, but it will shrink your waistline and help you reach your ideal weight.

Now, like I said before, you should keep far away from The Deadly Five. These include foods that contain hydrogenated fats, are high in sugar, are artificially processed, or are carb heavy. If you absolutely must have them in very small quantities until you can eventually wean yourself off of them for good. In regard to foods that are rich in saturated fats like butter, cheese, and animal fats, etc., make sure that you keep your consumption of them to smaller portions as well. Small portion sizes are the key in terms of feeling good as well as staying healthy in regard to these types of fatty foods. Don't overdo it. If your portions are reasonably small, then you will digest them without going into a mental fog. In my opinion and experience, there is nothing wrong with some natural fats such as butter if they are eaten in strict moderation because they are, at least, not processed. In my opinion, butter is better than margarine just by virtue of the fact that it is not processed. Understand that artificially processed foods are a part of The Deadly Five and it is very important to avoid them.

If you can stick to the 3/4ths rule for about 3 weeks, you may start to notice that you're getting used to it and not needing as much food to feel full after meals. It just takes some self-control not to overdo it and some discipline to regulate the portions accordingly. Now, as you decrease your portion size, it is also beneficial to increase the ratio of vegetables on your plate. My experience with fruits and vegetables is that the more you eat them, the more you end up liking them. I dare say that you may even get to a point where you crave vegetables! I know that sounds crazy, but for me this was true. Now, let's talk about the perfect ratio of food on your plate. The perfect ratio, or what I call, The Golden Ratio of types of foods on your plate should be:

The Golden Ratio (on your plate)

- 60% Vegetables or Fruit

- 20% Whole Grain Carbs or Beans

- 20% Fish or Lean Meat (or vegetarian-protein for vegans and vegetarians)

If you stick to The Golden Ratio, then you are in the sweet spot for feeling good after a meal. Remember to combine this with the 3/4ths full rule for best effect.

Diet Rule Number 4: Whole grain foods and beans

This diet rule pertains to your consumption of carbohydrates. The rule is very simple. It stipulates that the more your stomach needs to break something down, the better it is for you, and the better you will feel after eating it. Meaning, brown is better than white whether it be bread, pasta, or rice. And whole grain is always the way to go. Get into the habit of eating whole grain carbs, and you will feel consistently better. It is important to note that whole grains are good for your heart health as well as a host of other things. One scientific publication concludes that,

"This meta-analysis provides further evidence that whole grain intake is associated with a reduced risk of coronary heart disease, cardiovascular disease, and total cancer, and mortality from all causes, respiratory diseases, infectious diseases, diabetes, and all non-cardiovascular, non-cancer causes. These findings support dietary guidelines that recommend increased intake of whole grain to reduce the risk of chronic diseases and premature mortality"(Aune et al.).

In addition to this, whole grains do not cause the spikes in blood sugar that non-whole grains like refined white flour do. This shows that they are a far better choice when it comes to your diet. These spikes in blood sugar cause your brain to go on a roller-coaster ride that is harmful to your neurons. We will discuss this concept in more detail when we talk about sugar later on in an upcoming diet rule. In a lot of ways, non-whole grain carbs have a similar effect on your brain and body as sugar does. For this reason, you must try your best to consume whole grains as an alternative to refined white flour.

Diet Rule Number 5: Fiber

Diet rule number 5 is all about incorporating more fiber into your diet. Vegetables, beans, legumes, and whole grain foods are all a good source of fiber that will keep your digestive system running well. One of the reasons I recommend that 60% of your plate should be vegetables, is that you will get your fiber very easily that way. When you eat foods like fruits, vegetables, and beans, you get the sufficient amount of fiber that you need for your gut to function in a healthy way. When we discuss probiotics in an upcoming step, you will see how fiber is incredibly important for the regulation of your gut bacteria. That bacteria, in turn, regulates and creates everything from your neurotransmitters, to the vitamins in your system. A healthy gut, therefore, can result in the sustained improvement of your mood and health, and it all starts with fiber.

In order for you to get more fiber in your diet, you will need to start eating the following foods:

The Fantastic Fiber-Five

- Fruits

- Vegetables

- Nuts and Seeds

- Beans and Legumes

- Whole Grains – Bran, Oats, and Cereal

A regular and sustained intake of dietary fiber has been proven to be beneficial for the heart, the digestive system, as well as keeping diabetes at bay. The best things about eating fiber rich foods are that they do not cause a spike in blood sugar, and they provide sustained energy throughout the day. They have also been attributed to aging well. One study followed adults over the age of 49 for ten years and concluded that the more the fiber intake, the higher the chances of aging well and warding off disease (Gopinath et al.). What could be better than aging without illness? I always try to have beans for lunch in order to get an energy boost before a workout. Beans are an excellent way to get energy-rich fiber foods into your system without a spike in insulin. A small amount of beans can fill you up, and you can have sustained energy for hours afterward. The best thing about beans is their fiber, which makes them an excellent source of carbs.

In regard to my diet, I now swap beans for whole grain carbs as much as I can. This has been a great move in order for me to get the appropriate amount of fiber in my diet. I would suggest that for half of your meals you consume whole grains, and for half of them, you consume beans.

Diet Rule Number 6: Cut out sugar

One of the ways that you can immediately feel better is to cut out refined sugar, or anything that contains it, from your diet. Sugar has a terrible way of taking your brain on a roller-coaster ride. When you first have it, you peak and feel almost euphoric. Then, as you probably know, you crash and burn and wonder why you feel low thereafter. The dangerous thing about sugar is that the more you have it, the more you crave it. Getting rid of it is like kicking an addiction. At first, it is hard and uncomfortable, but once you have maintained a habit of not giving in to it, you will find yourself free of it and happier as a result. It takes discipline. One of the hardest things for me to quit was sugar because of the sheer fact that it is so prevalent. The boss brings in donuts, your grandma makes cookies, and then there is pumpkin pie on Thanksgiving and birthday cake for everyone's birthday! It's everywhere in our society not to mention pop, candy, and chocolate. The temptation is always around. And saying no to it often makes you look and sound like a killjoy. After all, people revel in the idea of eating together and celebrating together, and they often do it with sugar. When you say no to the sugar, you sometimes feel like you are saying no to them as a person. You must stay strong. Don't cave in. Be an example. You will find yourself in a much better place, mentally, if you cut it out. There have been numerous studies in regard to the damaging effects of sugar on the brain and its negative effects on mood. One particularly good article on the negative effects of sugar on the brain was published online by Psychology Today. They say that too much sugar can be very bad for the brain; hurting your attention span, short-term memory, and affecting mood in a negative way. They go on to say that, refined sugar slows down neural communication, blocks membranes, increases free radicals, interferes with synapses, makes it harder to think clearly, and can damage neurons ("Why Sugar Leads to a Brain Low").

When you free yourself from sugar, you truly free yourself from a damaging narcotic-like substance. Once you cut sugar out, your body will start to begin to naturally optimize the way it metabolizes food, and some great things happen: your body starts naturally stabilizing your blood sugar when you eat, and you begin to enjoy natural foods more. This happens to your taste buds. By quitting something that is so sweet, like refined sugar, you begin to appreciate the taste of foods like fresh fruits, with their natural sugars. When you stop sweetening things with sugar, your threshold for sweet things re-adjusts itself so that you don't need something to be as sweet for you to experience pleasure from eating it. I remember when I hit my 8-month mark of quitting sugar and I decided to have a small bite of pumpkin pie. It was like a punch in the face and entirely way too sweet. I had grown accustomed to the natural sugars of fruits, and when I had the refined version, I found it to be way too overbearing. Having said that, it was very pleasurable and even addictive in that I found myself craving it again the next day. For the first time in many months, I actually craved sugar and wanted more. This showed me that sugar is no different than substances like nicotine, in that your body feels like it needs it after you've had a taste. When you cut out sugar, you will find that you not only feel better and think clearer, but you will eventually free yourself from the addiction. That is worth the struggle of saying no to it on a daily basis.

Quitting sugar is not as hard as you think. All it takes is some discipline to say no to it for about three weeks or so. After that tough, three-week period, you will find that you don't even miss it. Your body and brain readjust, and you stop craving it. There will be certain times when you will want something that contains refined sugar. Resist it. If you do, I promise, you will soar in terms of your brain health and mood. Just be strong and kick the habit for three weeks, after that you will get to the next level in terms of your health.

Also, whatever you do, if you cut out the sugar, do not replace it with artificial sweeteners of any kind. These fall into the category of processed foods and are detrimental to a healthy diet in many ways. On the Scientific American website, there is an article that sums it up well. It concludes that artificial sweeteners change the way your body breaks sugar down and harms the healthy bacteria in your gut. They also say that artificial sweeteners interfere with your metabolism and are linked to Type-2 diabetes. (Shell et al.). It's crucial to cut out all artificial sweeteners and sugar out of your diet, but if you absolutely must have something sweet, try honey. I often sweeten things with a very small bit of honey. From my own personal experience, I find honey does not give me the sugar crash that refined sugar does. I've always thought that honey is somewhat magical in that it is very sweet but has more of a positive effect on blood sugar than sugar does. In one article published in the Journal of Diabetes & Metabolic Disorders, the researchers conclude that using diabetes drugs in conjunction with consuming honey is beneficial for glycemic control, the promulgation of an antioxidant effect, and the decrease in oxidative damage to the body

(Erejuwa). These effects are believed to be promoted by the antioxidant mechanism of honey. Honey is known to be rich in antioxidants and even antimicrobial. There is a reason why honey never goes bad. It has everything to do with the fact that honey has a strong and stable molecular structure. Try making the switch from other sweeteners to honey. You won't regret it.

Diet Rule Number 7: The super smoothie

Once I started changing the little things with my diet, I felt better on a daily basis. I took a chance and applied for a new job. This particular job was a lot more challenging than my previous one, but I decided to push myself to take it on and do something a bit more challenging even though I was still not 100%. I found that my new diet kept me alert and awake all throughout the day during work. I began to do better at work as a result, and slowly, over time, my strong and boisterous personality started to reappear again. My diet had everything to do with that. I was beginning to see the fruits of my labor. I realized that all the little things that I was doing each and every day were getting me to this new healthy place. I would have to keep it up and make it all a part of my daily life if I wanted it to continue. I didn't skip my walks or runs. I was diligent about eating right. I would meditate and practice diaphragmatic breathing every day. I also kept taking the omega-3s every day. I was nearing a tipping point in terms of feeling like myself again. I was at the point where I would have about five good days a week and about two bad days. Those bad days were still hard to get through, but I could see the light at the end of the tunnel.

What eventually helped me to get to the next level (in terms of not only feeling better every day but feeling consistently good throughout each day) was my new dedication to drinking a super smoothie every day. What I discovered was that smoothies helped immensely in terms of my energy levels. The particular smoothie I drank every day was my own creation made up of organic fruits and vegetables. As I drank it throughout my days, it started to do something I never dreamed of. It made me feel better than I ever felt – even before my depression. I discovered that the reason smoothies are so effective is because they are powerful combinations of many good ingredients. When these potent ingredients are combined and consumed together, they shock your body into a healthy state. The sheer fact that I was ingesting a punch of vitamins and antioxidants in one serving was the key. The ingredients are very important, and this particular smoothie that I am about to tell you about truly made the difference in my daily diet and my daily mood. It is great, in that, it contains brain super foods that will reduce inflammation as well as give you a full spectrum of nutrition. First, you will need a good blender, and second, you will need an open mind. You must be willing to try something new and somewhat outrageous. My super smoothie contains fruits and vegetables that are rich in color (which we will talk about in a bit). It is packed with vitamins and nutrients and also has extremely effective anti-inflammatory properties. Many scientists now point to the fact that depression may very well be an inflammatory disease and that the more anti-inflammatory foods we consume, the better we feel when we are fighting it. Here is the recipe for my magical super-smoothie.

The Super Smoothie

- One small beet

- One banana

- 12 Oz of coconut water (not from concentrate)

- One medium piece of raw ginger

- One cup frozen organic frozen blueberries

- One cup frozen organic mangos

- Two handfuls of fresh organic spinach or spring mix

- One tablespoon of organic wheat grass powder

Color, color, color! If you look at the ingredients

of this smoothie, you will see that, as I said before, it contains fruits and vegetables that are rich in color like beets and blueberries. As a general rule, you must try to eat fruits and vegetables that are rich in color. The reason is that these foods possess high amounts of antioxidants and phytochemicals, which have been shown to be integral to preventing disease. In an article in the publication Molecule, they sum it up this way,

"Overproduction of oxidants (reactive oxygen species and reactive nitrogen species) in the human body is responsible for the pathogenesis of some diseases. The scavenging of these oxidants is thought to be an effective measure to depress the level of oxidative stress of organisms. It has been reported that intake of vegetables and fruits is inversely associated with the risk of many chronic diseases, and antioxidant phytochemicals in vegetables and fruits are considered to be responsible for these health benefits. Antioxidant phytochemicals can be found in many foods and medicinal plants, and play an important role in the prevention and treatment of chronic diseases caused by oxidative stress" (Zhang).

I cannot stress enough the importance of filling your diet with anti-inflammatory foods. The ginger in the smoothie will take some getting used to but is incredibly powerful when it comes decreasing inflammation. Nothing reduces inflammation quite like ginger, and once you get used to it, you will find that it is very addictive in the best possible way. In fact, I found, I often craved having ginger in my smoothie because it made me feel so great immediately after I had it. In terms of the taste, the frozen blueberries, mangos, and bananas add a natural sweetness that makes this smoothie delicious. It tastes more like a fruit smoothie than a veggie one.

I promise you, if you begin to have this super smoothie twice a day, it will help you to not only feel better, but it will help you to excel in your daily life. I found that as soon as I started having it daily, after a month or so, the days in which I had bad depression were reduced, and my higher brain functions like creativity simultaneously went through the roof. My energy levels also skyrocketed, and I was able to accomplish twice as much at work. Within a few short months, I received a big promotion. It simply made me feel great every time I had one and helped me to thrive. It also helped me on days where my stress levels were high as I had a lot more of those types of days after I took on more at work. The crazy part was that no matter how stressful it got, I could handle it all with ease. I even asked my boss for more work! It really took me to a place where I was functioning at my best.

I would make sure to have it after my workouts as well. I would just add a couple of raw eggs to it for protein or organic protein powder. Do not be afraid of the natural sugars that are in smoothies. From my experience, they did not spike my blood sugar in any way, and I never felt a sugar crash from the natural sugars of fruits. Please don't let anyone tell you that natural sugars in fruits are bad. Unless you have a condition that is exacerbated by fruit sugars, they are not detrimental to your diet. You need lots of fruits and vegetables if you want to have a healthy diet. I've never gained any additional weight from the natural sugars in fruits or vegetables, even though I was consuming two or three large glasses of fruit filled smoothies every day. Natural sugars have never contributed to any type of sugar crash for me and have always been a good source of natural energy.

In many ways, this smoothie helped me get over the worst part of my depression. The bottom line was that it got me to start feeling great on a consistent basis. I can truly say that my healing was accelerated, and I was easily able to reach the next level of my well-being. You can make your own super smoothie with the fruits and vegetables that you love. There are tons of great recipes out there. Just make sure always to add ginger, and ensure that the fruits and vegetables have lots of color. Also, do not add any sugar or sweeteners to it.

Diet Rule Number 8: Healthy fats

Healthy fats, such as monounsaturated fats and polyunsaturated fats, are essential for the healthy functioning of your brain. The simple reason is that your brain needs these types of fats, including omega-3s, in order to survive and thrive. Not only do you need healthy fats in your diet for your brain, but they can be beneficial for the maintenance of your heart health as well. The jury is still out on whether or not saturated fats are indeed harmful to you or not. Many health practitioners still recommend limiting your intake of animal-based saturated fats like butter and fats from meat sources. In my experience, as I've said before, these types of fats are okay as long as they are consumed in strict moderation. The research usually states that too much of them can be dangerous. I tend to stick to monounsaturated fats like olive oil and avocado oil and polyunsaturated fats like omega-3s and sunflower oil. I also eat plant-based saturated fats like coconut oil. These are my go-to healthy fats and are all a must for a healthy and balanced diet. The sole reason I limit my consumption of animal-based saturated fats like butter, and any type of animal fat, is because they make me feel a bit groggy, foggy, and sleepy after I eat them.

Below is a list of excellent foods that you can consume if you want a good source of healthy fats.

Healthy Fats

- Olive oil

- Coconut oil

- Flaxseed oil

- Avocado oil

- Hemp seed oil

- Fish oil

- Nuts

- Seeds

- Seafood

- Avocados

Healthy fats have been shown to decrease your weight naturally as well as reduce your waistline. These fats are essential to a balanced diet, and once you incorporate them in moderation, they can definitely be a delicious addition to your diet regime.

Remember, stay away from any fats that are hydrogenated in any way. When they are partially or fully hydrogenated, these types of otherwise healthy oils turn into trans-fats. These types of fats are found in all types of pre-made foods and show up in cakes, cookies, chips, processed and fast foods. There is now evidence that trans fats not only affect the heart but may cause cancer. One study discusses the fact that trans fats have been proven, by the scientific community, to be very risky for heart health and that a few studies have found that they have cancer-promoting effects on the body (Fujii et al.). Be diligent about these dangerous fats and do your research as well as read your labels. My simple rule is that if it contains trans fats, then I don't eat it.

Diet Rule Number 9: Consumption of turmeric

By now, you can probably tell that I am very passionate about you incorporating a smoothie, like the one above, in your fight against depression. Like I said before, the smoothies were definitely a step in the right direction when it came to my intake of anti-inflammatory foods and foods with color. Trust me when I say, the more anti-inflammatory foods you eat, the better. One particular anti-inflammatory food or more accurately, spice, is turmeric. The statistics show that the population of India does not suffer Alzheimer's disease to the degree that the population of North America or Europe suffer from it. This is because of turmeric. The spice that is prevalent in curry is a magical anti-inflammatory agent that guards and protects the brain and keeps it healthy. If you have ever come into contact with turmeric, you will notice that it stains your fingers yellow. Well, this very same property of color saturation is what makes it so good at protecting your brain and keeps it functioning well. This quality of saturation is exhibited when it crosses the blood brain barrier and seeps in to protect your brain like nothing else can. In a recent study, it was proven that curcumin, the active ingredient in turmeric, is an anti-inflammatory by inhibiting the very molecules that cause inflammation (Chainani-Wu). It is this anti-inflammatory effect it has on the brain that makes turmeric so good for you.

When consuming turmeric, you must ensure that you are taking it with healthy fats. The curcumin in turmeric is strictly fat-soluble and needs to be consumed with fats in order to be absorbed into your body. For the fats, you can use the good fats in the previous diet rule, like olive oil, coconut oil, and flaxseed oil as well as any type of saturated fats like cream, milk, or butter. I would tend to stick to the healthier vegetable fats. Having said this, I regularly stir in a spice mix, with turmeric, cinnamon, and ground ginger into my daily cup of tea along with cream. This not only spices my tea up in a great way, but it allows me to digest and consume turmeric.

Turmeric is definitely in my daily diet arsenal against depression. As soon as I started consuming it regularly, I noticed that it had a positive effect on reducing stress and keeping my mind clear and sharp. For this reason, I will continue to consume it for the rest of my life. I often sprinkle turmeric on my scrambled eggs along with some chopped onions – which makes for a delicious meal in the morning. I also add it to spice up some breast of chicken that I stir-fry or marinate. It is great as an ingredient in curries of course, and it can even be added to a smoothie, provided you add some coconut oil to it as well. One incredible way to incorporate turmeric into your diet is a spice mixture that my mom saw on CNN when she was watching Dr. Sanjay Gupta. I call it Mom's Mix, though. It consists of equal parts of turmeric, ground ginger, and Ceylon cinnamon. Mom's Mix is great for oatmeal, cinnamon toast, or as an additive to teas and coffee (I'll talk about that in a bit). This mixture is so delicious that I have to have it with my steel cut oats every morning along with some coconut oil. I affectionately call it Heavenly Oats (recipe to follow). Just make sure to use Ceylon cinnamon and not cassia cinnamon (the latter of which is found in most grocery stores). The cassia variety is more prevalent but has a much higher amount of a substance called coumarin. Coumarin, in high to medium doses, has been found to be toxic to the liver and the kidney. I personally felt a little ill when I consumed too much of the cassia type of cinnamon, whereas when I consumed the Ceylon variety of cinnamon, I felt no adverse effects. You can find the Ceylon cinnamon at your neighbourhood health food store or organic market. It is a little more expensive, but it is totally worth it. Another amazing ingredient in Mom's Mix is ground ginger, which is also great for reducing inflammation. The triple threat of turmeric, ground ginger, and Ceylon cinnamon makes for a delicious and powerful additive to foods. The best way that I have probably used this mixture is as an additive to my coffee or tea. I just add about a half teaspoon of the triple mixture along with cream or milk to my coffee or tea. I am now ruined as a result because I cannot have my coffee or tea without it. If you are going to add it to your coffee or tea, just make sure to add cream or milk with a little bit of fat in it (min 2%) as turmeric is fat-soluble. You can also add almond milk if you want to use a non-dairy option, as it contains fats for the turmeric to properly dissolve in.

Below are a couple of recipes that I came up with that use the triple mixture of turmeric, ground ginger and Ceylon cinnamon (Mom's Mix) in them. The first is a wonderful, natural, tea concoction that I came up called Heavenly Tea. The best thing about this hot drink is that it tastes absolutely amazing – hence the name. It provides you with sustained energy for hours after you drink it. It is based on the concept behind bulletproof coffee. If you haven't heard of bulletproof coffee, it is black coffee blended with a small amount of grass fed butter and medium chain triglyceride oil. Bulletproof coffee is purported to be a natural energy drink. The claim is that it gives you sustained energy, without a crash, when all of those ingredients are blended together. It is all based on the idea that some kind of special bond occurs between the coffee and the butter. Now, I tried bulletproof coffee and found that for me the claims were somewhat true – it did give me a high amount of energy, but I also found that I was way too jittery after I drank it and didn't like the way it made me feel. I was also a little hesitant about blending a small square of butter into my coffee on a daily basis because of the intake of saturated fat. I, therefore, decided to make a similar drink, which I call Heavenly Tea. I make it with black tea, coconut oil, honey, and that same mixture of turmeric, ground ginger, and Ceylon cinnamon (Mom's Mix). What I ended up discovering was a drink that tasted amazing and was great for natural energy. It also did not give me a sugar crash and was absolutely delicious. When I began drinking this tea regularly, I noticed many benefits such as the fact that I was able to focus on my work incredibly well. It would also give me a nuclear-boost before activities like running, hiking, and weight training. I would drink it before I went out and hence had no need for alcohol to get-me-going. It was a great addition to my diet in that I was able to get my healthy fats like coconut oil. I was also able to consume turmeric on a regular basis, which was my initial intention in the first place.

Another recipe that uses Mom's Mix is what I mentioned earlier: Heavenly Oats. This breakfast meal will not only give you a great daily source of fiber but also contains good fats as well as turmeric. It is a triple threat when it comes to a healthy meal. You may sweeten it with some honey or even a little bit of organic maple syrup for a delicious treat.

Below are the recipes for my Heavenly Tea, Heavenly Oats, and another great drink called Maple Spiced Coffee, all of which have turmeric in them:

Heavenly Tea

- Black tea (hot)

- 1-teaspoon coconut oil

- 1-teaspoon milk

- ½ teaspoon of Mom's Mix (Mixture of

even parts turmeric, ground ginger, Ceylon

- cinnamon)

- ½ teaspoon honey

*Blend all ingredients in a blender for 20 seconds to make a super drink

Heavenly Oats

- Steel cut oats boiled in water (stovetop or microwave)

- 1-tablespoon coconut oil

- ½ teaspoon of Mom's Mix (mixture of even parts turmeric, ground ginger, and

- Ceylon cinnamon)

- One-tablespoon organic maple syrup or honey

Spiced Maple Coffee

- Black coffee (hot)

- 2 tablespoons of cream

- ½ Teaspoon of Mom's Mix (Mixture of even parts turmeric, ground ginger, Ceylon cinnamon)

- ½ teaspoon organic maple syrup

Try these out! Who knows, you may actually love them. The best part is that they are a great way to consume turmeric into your daily diet. That in itself is worth the try.

Diet Rule Number 10: Swap red meat for fish

As my diet became more and more healthy, by

eating more fruits and vegetables, I found that I naturally gravitated towards eating more fish. I discovered that one easy way to feel better throughout the week was to increase my intake of fish while simultaneously decreasing my intake of red meat. The main reason was that after I ate fish, I always felt sharp and light on my feet. Fish was always great for my mood after I ate it. Now, if you are a vegetarian, this part of the book may not really apply to you. If you eat meat, like I do, then this shift can really change things for the better in regard to your diet. When you make this switch, you may notice that you feel more nimble and mentally agile. Just be careful to limit your intake of fish to 2-3 times a week. There are some trace amounts of heavy metals in certain big fish like tuna that can build up in your system and may be harmful after prolonged periods of too much consumption. It is not a bad idea to get your family doctor to test the metals in your blood once every six months if you are consuming a lot of fish. One supplement that is great for this is chlorella. It is one of the most popular supplements in Japan because of how much fish the population there consumes. Chlorella is a single-celled green algae that is great for absorbing and removing heavy metals from your body naturally. Coincidentally, it is also a brain superfood that does everything from give you more energy, to improve your mental concentration. It is also great in that it can improve the appearance of your skin and also naturally increases the beneficial bacteria in your gut. It is a super food and should be taken whether you eat fish or not. We will be covering supplements that help with depression as well as beneficial bacteria later on in this book. One reputable health and medical website breaks it down very well when they say that, chlorella rids the body of heavy metals like lead and mercury as well as increases beneficial bacteria in your gut. It has also been known to slow down aging and help with digestion ("Chlorella").

The best thing about chlorella is that it is a whole food so you can't really take too much. I take it after every meal and it makes me feel great. It also makes me feel safe about consuming more fish during the week.

Diet Rule Number 11: Green tea

The last thing that I wanted to include in this very important diet section is green tea. You have probably read or heard about the many benefits of green tea. From its antioxidant properties, because of its high concentration of polyphenols, to its anti-cancer claims. It has also been linked to promoting weight loss. Green tea is a wonder. It has been known to help the heart, skin, and even the brain. One study found that green tea actually had antidepressant qualities. They concluded that because of its extracts, green tea consumption could restore normal behaviour by reducing the oxidative stress in the body as well as promoting an internal, antioxidant form of defense (Lorenzo). This stuff is good for your brain and can help you to fight depression. It has also been shown to help you burn fat. There are great Chinese and Japanese varieties, and they can make you feel good if you consume them on a regular basis. Green tea also doesn't have as much caffeine as coffee and can be a better caffeinated drink that doesn't make you jittery. It can often be a good replacement for coffee. Many people I know have swapped it out for coffee in the mornings. This swap may be a bit hard at first, but you may find that if you try it, after a few days, you will get used to the change.

The benefits of green tea are touted everywhere from diet books to many health websites, and the information on why it is great is everywhere. Green tea is often recommended, by health practitioners, as a tonic in order to stay healthy. One particular website on nutrition outlines and illustrates the benefits of green tea. They point out that it contains flavonoids, polyphenols, and catechins that are antioxidant in nature and can reduce free radicals as well as protect your body's cells. They also point out that green tea contains a natural anti-anxiety promoting ingredient called l-theanine. Along with all of this, they say that green tea is great for burning fat and boosting metabolism. These are all great benefits that have been proven over the years about green tea ("10 Proven Benefits of Green Tea"). That is a lot of good things all in one shot! And once again, we have a food that is anti-inflammatory and antioxidant-rich. Green tea can be good for your depression too because of l-theanine. I have always found it to have a very surprisingly refreshing effect on my mood immediately after I drink it. I have also found that my skin looks great as a result of drinking it as well.

You should be aware that if you are on certain drugs, you may need to be careful if you drink too much green tea. There have been some studies that show that if you are on antipsychotics or mood stabilizers, too much green tea can interfere with them and cause them to be less effective. That can get you into trouble. The University of Maryland Medical Center website states in their article, Possible Interactions With: Green Tea, that the popular anti-psychotic drug, Clozapine, may be less effective if taken after drinking green tea. Of course, as said before, always make sure to consult your doctor with any new dietary changes, and research any potential drug interactions before taking on anything new.

How your Diet will make you Thrive.

Life is unpredictable. When you have good food in your stomach, you can deal with problems and stress in a much better way. As long as you stay away from the big no-no's, like The Deadly Five, which include processed foods, hydrogenated fats, and refined sugar, you should be on the right track. I want to repeat once again that the key, for me, was limiting the type of foods I ate as well as limiting the amounts of food I ate. You may need to eventually cut out the high-fat foods altogether and only have them on an occasional basis. You may also find out that when you overdo it and eat bad foods or too much food, that you may pay for it by going into a food-coma. My advice to you is to gradually make these changes. Just remember that if you try to cut all types of bad food out of your life, all at once, your body and brain may go into shock, and you will not succeed. Gradually make little changes, and eventually over a long period of time, you can start swapping out the bad for the good. Don't be an extremist when it comes to your diet, or you may end up rebelling against the whole thing and end up not doing any of it. You don't want to be in a place where you cannot make any changes at all because the prospect of change seems too painful to undertake. Start out by making small changes and incremental changes. See what foods you like and which healthy foods you enjoy. Increase those in your diet. This is the way to succeed.

Start by beginning to test things out for yourself.

Eat certain foods, and keep track of how they make you feel afterward. This is the best way, to truly see, what foods make you feel better and what foods make you feel worse. Start noticing. I would eat impulsively before, and it would almost always get me into trouble. I would have sugary sweets or something that was highly processed or something rich and fatty. As a result, I would feel horrible for at least a few hours afterward – foggy, sluggish, and tired. The funny part is that I kept doing this over and over until finally one day, I decided to stop repeating the insanity. I don't know when it was exactly, but one day, I went through the process of imagining how I would feel if I ate the junk, before I even ate it. When I did this, I visualized feeling terrible after eating the bad food. That did it. It finally worked. I didn't go through with it in the first place. It was like I saw the truth of it before I even did it. From then on, a shift happened within me, and I started to consciously think about the decisions I had made about food before I acted on them. With practice, I got better and better at it until my self-control became very strong when it came to food decisions. When I did want something that was unhealthy like chips –chips were always my worst craving – I would have such a small amount of them that they would not affect me very much. The truth is, though, when I stopped eating those unhealthy foods, I stopped craving them altogether. When I stopped craving them, then I was not in their sphere of influence. I was forging new ground, on a new path, to a new level of health. You can reach this level when you start to slowly gain the necessary self-control over certain unhealthy foods. Foods like pop, donuts, chips, etc. When you do gain this control, then you will begin to soar in terms of how you feel from day to day. When I began to feel incredibly good, as a result of constant good choices, there was no way I was going to go back to those bad habits. I had created new habits that were empowering me and helping me to achieve my diet goals as well as my life goals. Throughout this process, my depression started to get better. That was all the positive feedback I needed to keep it going. My advice to you is to start these new habits and keep them going. See how long you can do it. How many days in a row can you keep it going? Keep the momentum going, and you will plow through your old habits and forge new ones out of steel.

How to Break the Bad-Food-

Habit

Begin to take stock of how you feel after you eat certain foods. Remember how they make you feel right after you've eaten them. Track what foods make you feel good and which ones make you feel bad. You have the ability to find out which foods work for you and which don't. For the ones that don't work, visualize how they make you feel bad before you eat them. No matter how delicious you may think they are, it is not worth the feeling afterward. This will help you to stop yourself from eating them in the first place. Nothing is worse than being in a mental fog where you feel sleepy for the rest of the day. Stop the negative cycle. Food has the ability to depress or elate. Once you visualize how they make you feel before eating them, then you will win. When you exercise this self-control over a bad choice, then choose a better, healthier option in its place that you will enjoy. I assure you that when you start choosing healthier foods, the effects will compound and help you in terms of the way you feel. You will then find yourself building momentum, and pretty soon you will begin to feel great on a consistent basis.

Step 6 - Effective Supplements and Vitamins

"To every problem, there is a most simple solution."

-Agatha Christie

Supplements and vitamins can be very powerful

in terms of making you feel better. In my experience, there were many times when certain supplements worked faster and better when it came to making me feel like myself again than anything else did. If you are able to find the right ones that work for you, then you have an opportunity for feeling better relatively quickly. The main supplements we have already talked about, like omega-3s and chlorella, are crucial to start right away for the benefits that we have already covered. The others I will outline here have their own benefits, and they can help you to do everything from mitigating stress, to reducing cognitive fog or fatigue.

One very powerful supplement that you can begin to take in order to eliminate cognitive fatigue is l-tyrosine. This complex amino acid is very inexpensive and should be taken on an empty stomach. Before I began taking this supplement, I always felt tired and foggy throughout the day. I had trouble keeping up with my girlfriend when we were engaged in conversations. My mind was just too slow and groggy, and I would often just stop talking and want to disengage. I often even had a strong urge to go to sleep during the day. The term, cognitive fatigue, perfectly explained how I felt most of the time during my depression. More and more, on bad depression days, I felt like I had to stop conversations because I was tired of talking and thinking. It was very scary to me because everyone had always seen me as being incredibly talkative when I was healthy. In my case, I also felt that I had a mental fog that just couldn't be lifted, and it felt as if I had a cloud over my head. Once I started to take a 500 mg dose of l-tyrosine every day, it felt like a miracle had happened with my clarity. I had more cognitive energy than ever before and became more talkative and engaged again. I felt so much better after a few weeks of taking it, that my friends and family remarked on how I had started to become myself again. It really allowed me to communicate better with my friends and family, and it helped me to turn a corner in my fight with depression.

Another supplement, that can be integral for reducing stress and increasing energy, is a good B vitamin. B vitamins can be crucial to helping you get better and stay better. They sometimes immediately make people, who are suffering from depression, feel better because of the fact that so many people are deficient in them. The good news is that they aren't that expensive.

Choose a brand that has the following types and dosages of B vitamins. A good B-complex should have close to the following dosages below:

- B1 – 50 mg

- B2 – 50 mg

- B3– 50 mg

- B5 – 50 mg

- B6 – 50 mg

- B12 – 50 mcg

- Biotin – 50 mcg

- Folate – 400 mcg

- Inositol – 50 mg

This mix is not overbearingly strong and can be taken daily. The key with B vitamins is dosing. There is a sweet spot in regard to how much to take. Since B vitamins are fat soluble, taking too much can be toxic to you. I found that with a good B complex, one is enough per day. B vitamins are crucial for the functioning of your brain. One article, in the publication Nutritional Neuroscience, concludes that certain supplements, like B vitamins and omega-3s, can stunt the onset and development of depression (Nabavi). I always find that the B complex I take calms me and makes me feel better when I am stressed. I still take one every day.

Now, let's talk about vitamin D. The truth is that vitamin D deficiency in North America, and much of the world, is a real problem. Depending on your skin tone, you need varying amounts of direct sunlight in order to produce this vitamin in your body. If you are very fair skinned, then that could mean twenty minutes of direct exposure to the sun per day. Dark skinned individuals, like me, need to have at least an hour of direct sun exposure daily. Now as you may know, in the North American winter months, this can be hard to accomplish. We often get mixed messages from health practitioners

232

about getting direct sun exposure and the information about the skin cancer risk associated with it is everywhere. Having said all of this, vitamin D deficiency is a real problem, and getting enough vitamin D remains incredibly crucial for the functioning of each of your cells. In terms of your brain, getting enough vitamin D is crucial. Scientific American states in their article Does Vitamin D Improve Brain Function that, low amounts of vitamin D in subjects' systems were correlated to negative performance in regard to cognitive tests. Those with low levels were two times more likely to be "cognitively impaired" than those with optimal levels. It also goes on to state that, vitamin D protects neurons and decreases inflammation (Welland). Here again, we have a supplement that reduces inflammation! In my experience, as soon I started supplementing with vitamin D, I began to see a change for the better in regard to my health. This had to do with the fact that I was able to fight inflammation with yet another proven anti-inflammatory agent.

More and more, people seem to be deficient in vitamin D. Dr. Steven Masley, an expert on diet and nutrition in regard to heart health, remarked in his PBS special that up to 95% of the population of the United States is deficient in vitamin D. The simple fact is that vitamin D is not only crucial for the functioning of your brain and heart but also helps to fight off autoimmune diseases and reduces the number of birth defects in pregnant women. In terms of depression and the brain, an article found in Annals of Rehabilitation Medicine concludes that depression in stroke patients was correlated to vitamin D deficiency (Kim et al.). Vitamin D cannot be discounted and needs to become a priority, as a preventative measure, for the battling of depression and the maintenance of overall health.

All of this information can at times seem overwhelming. It does seem like you need to remember to take a lot of supplements and always eat the right kind of foods in order to win this fight. I promise you, though, that they are all worth it. From my experience, it takes a confluence of actions in order to start gaining momentum. Once you do, you may just be on your way to feeling better each day as well as building the foundation of how to thrive on a daily basis. In my experience, vitamin D supplementation was definitely a big and easy solution. I would therefore strongly recommend

236

that you supplement with vitamin D. Most health sources, that I have researched, suggest a dose of no more than 2000 IU per day. This is the dosage that worked well for me. In my experience, the liquid form of vitamin D is the best. I like the D-drops in that they are easy to take and very bioavailable. I put it in my water or juice in the morning and can't even taste it. Make sure to add a vitamin D supplement to your diet if you are not getting enough direct sunlight. It will make all of the difference in your fight against depression and may ensure that your brain and body functions well in the years ahead.

Chlorella, l-tyrosine, B vitamins, vitamin D, and omega-3s have all been integral in regard to helping me fight my depression. Again, always consult your doctor about all of the supplements that you start, and see if they are a right fit for you. You want to make sure that there are no interactions with any drugs that you are taking, now or in the future. Nowadays, there are so many supplements out there, and they all make so many different claims. It can be hard to know which claims are factual and which are not. Do your own research. People with depression are often the most vulnerable to bad information because there is so much of it out there and they

are so desperate to feel better right away. Know

that there are no shortcuts. You will need to see

what works for you, first and foremost.

Step 7 - Probiotics

"Don't be too timid and squeamish about your

actions.

All life is an experiment. "

-Ralph Waldo Emerson

I could have very easily fit probiotics into the

diet section, but I didn't for a very important

reason. The reason is that I believe it to be one of the most important components of my success, in terms of battling mental illness. It rightfully deserves its own chapter. In the past, bacteria were mainly seen by the general public to be only a harmful thing because of the scary world of infectious diseases. Bad bacteria took over our consciousness because of our fear of it. The notion of beneficial bacteria was something that was not talked about very much, and mainstream health practitioners never touted it as a solution to any of our health problems. In the last ten years, there has been an almost exponential surge in research that has come

242

about in terms of the connection between our guts and our health. Everything from mental health to digestive health to overall well-being, beneficial bacteria is now considered a healthy solution to many of the diseases that plague us. The evidence and research on the subject have been extraordinary. Researchers have now shown that everything from the way we process vitamins, to the creation of our neurotransmitters, happens in our digestive system with the aid of bacteria. In fact, the bacteria in our bodies far outnumber our cells. We have about 10 trillion cells that make up our body, whereas we have 100 trillion living bacteria that live inside our bodies. Bacteria outnumber us tenfold. With that undeniable fact, the truth is, that we must cultivate and keep those good bacteria growing and thriving for the sake of our own health. We are symbiotically connected to these bacteria, and they are as much a part of who we are as our flesh and bones. We absolutely, therefore, need to cultivate the healthy beneficial bacteria in our guts. When we do this, the ecosystem that they live in, the microbiome, grows and thereby naturally aids our bodies to reduce inflammation. This process begins to fight depression and anxiety in a very natural way. In his book Brain Maker, Dr. David

244

Perlmutter outlines the research behind these facts and cites numerous studies to show how a healthy gut keeps our brains and bodies functioning well, and also aids in fighting diseases like depression and anxiety. He says succinctly,

"There are many types of anxiety disorders, just as there is a wide spectrum of depression, but the two conditions have a lot in common in terms of the state of gut bacteria. As with depression, anxiety is strongly related to the disruption of the gut microbiota. Numerous studies have found the same kinds of features in people with anxiety disorder as those with depression: Higher levels of inflammation in the gut"(86).

So, how do we get the right kind of bacteria to flourish in our guts? And how do the bacteria reduce inflammation in our guts? Well, it has a lot to do with what we eat and our diet; more fruits, more vegetables, and more fiber, which are called prebiotics. Then, more infusions of probiotics so that the microbiome can flourish. When it does, it creates that all-important anti-inflammatory state in our bodies. We will get to the nuts and bolts of this in a minute, but first I want to talk about how probiotics have changed my life.

When I first started to eat foods with probiotics, it felt amazing. I was very happy to discover that beneficial bacteria not only melted away a lot of my fear and anxiety, it also made me feel about ten years younger and gave me the energy of a teenager. Of course, all of this was dependent on my diet and the amount of prebiotics that I was eating. Like I said before, prebiotics are foods that you eat in order for the beneficial bacteria to thrive. These plant-based, fiber rich foods were the key. Anything with natural cellulose-based fiber. When I consumed these types of foods like fruits, vegetables, beans, and whole grains, the healthy bacteria in my belly would consume them and would thrive. This not only melted away my fear and anxiety but made me feel great as a result of reducing inflammation in my gut. The process is involved and complex, but it seemed pretty easy. It healed my fear and anxiety faster than anything else. I learned that I must be diligent in my consumption of fruits and vegetables. I also learned that if I ate foods that were rich in saturated or hydrogenated fat, sugar, or simple carbs, it polluted my microbiome and the "bad" bacteria could start to overtake the good. If you eat food like The Deadly Five, you start to lose the healthy benefits of good bacteria. Sounds like an epic battle, doesn't it? In these instances, you create an inflammatory gut. As you can begin to see now, everything is interconnected. The healthier your diet, the better off you are in every way.

The good news is that you can easily and inexpensively create a healthy microbiome, or happy gut, with a few small changes in your diet. First off, you will need to eat more fermented foods like sauerkraut, pickles, or Kimchi and also eat more foods with natural probiotics in them like yogurt, kefir, or kombucha. Second, you will need to eat more fruits and vegetables in order for the bacteria to feed on and thrive. Remember The Magnificent Seven? Simple as that.

When I started eating prebiotics and followed it by eating probiotics, I started to feel great every day. It also started helping me to see what foods would grow the beneficial bacteria and what wouldn't. This was a very helpful feedback loop in teaching me what to eat on a regular basis. What I ultimately learned is that if I wanted to keep the good feeling going, I had to eat plenty of fruits, vegetables, beans, and fiber rich foods. In a lot of ways, what I was doing was cultivating a healthy microbiome that would not only help my daily moods but also give me more energy. I also discovered that with my new healthy microbiome, every time I had yogurt or Kimchi or anything with beneficial bacteria in it, it would melt away my stress and give me a boost of energy. A natural boost, without the aid of caffeine or sugar. It was like a revelation! My caffeine intake went down, and I soon found myself consuming more probiotic foods. I actually did not need caffeine in the mornings any longer because I would have yogurt and it would wake me up and give me the energy I needed to get going. It seemed miraculous.

Another part of this puzzle of interconnectedness is the fact that if you eat fruits and vegetables that are free of pesticides, they are better for your gut. Pesticides are not only harmful to your cells, but they kill the beneficial bacteria in your microbiome. Eating organic may be a bit more expensive, but the benefits for your microbiome far outweigh the cost. The good news is that organic produce is becoming more and more widely available at regular supermarkets, and their prices are getting to be on par with non-organic produce.

Start eating fermented foods, and you will see the benefits. If you are grossed out by the idea of eating or drinking foods with bacteria in them, I implore you to fight through it and push yourself outside your comfort zone. You will need to start to introduce these bacteria into your system very slowly and gradually to see the benefits. Once they establish themselves in your system, you will feel better. Do your research on probiotic foods. You will find that they are not only good for a healthy gut but can be a source of naturally occurring vitamins and even essential hormones. For example, kefir (a probiotic fermented milk drink) contains a great natural source of vitamin D and also has a naturally high amount of melatonin. Melatonin is the hormone that regulates your circadian rhythms. In fact, I drink kefir at night before I sleep and have found that my sleep has improved as a result. I also had a friend who struggled with insomnia and it helped her to fall asleep at night because of the natural amounts of melatonin. We will talk about the importance of sleep and melatonin in an upcoming chapter, but for now, make a mental note that kefir can help you in regard to your sleep cycle.

One last thing that can greatly help you build a healthy microbiome is raw, unfiltered apple cider vinegar. It can help you to keep a balanced pH in your stomach, while simultaneously adding healthy bacteria to your microbiome.

It is important to mention that, as your intakes of natural probiotic sources like kombucha, kefir, and Kimchi increases, you may at times be at risk for increasing and accumulating the amount of yeast in your system. Make sure to not overdo it. Stick to the daily-recommended portions of these probiotic foods, every day. Absolutely stay away from yeast heavy beverages like non-alcoholic beer as well as malt beverages when you're drinking kombucha or kefir on a regular basis. Yeast overgrowth can be horrible, and it is important to keep a good balance in your gut. Just be careful. A healthy microbiome is very important but listening to your body is more important. No matter how good you feel consuming these probiotic foods, more is not necessarily better. Find healthy portions that work for you.

Start cultivating your healthy gut right away. Below is a list of probiotic foods and beverages that will naturally build up your healthy microbiome and help to improve your mood.

Probiotic Foods

- Kefir

- Sauerkraut

- Kimchi

- Pickles (Any kind without sugar)

- Yogurt

- Tempeh

- Fermented Foods

- Raw Unfiltered Apple Cider Vinegar

- Probiotic Supplements

- Kombucha

*Seventh Chapter

Breather

Hey, you've made it this far, and you're doing great! If you are enjoying the book, then please take a moment and give it a review on Amazon. I would really appreciate it, and your review will help get this book to others who can use it to get better. Cheers.

Step 8 - Pharmaceuticals

"It's hard to beat a person who never gives up."

-Babe Ruth

In recent years, there has been a widespread demonization of pharmaceutical drugs in the alternative media circles which has bled into the mainstream consciousness. It has much to do with the perception that drug companies only care about profits and are pushing their agenda without regard for people's safety or well-being. This, unfortunately, is true in rare cases but has become a dangerous assumption and a broad generalization. As with many subjects, once you get past the hype, the truth is very different. The simple fact is that drugs and drug companies save millions of lives every day. In reality, without modern drugs, our society, and our civilization would be in a lot of trouble. It could be argued that modern drugs are the very reason our life expectancies have gone up over the last 40 years. We often take for granted the ease at which we get better when we take them. The fact remains that the amount of research that has gone into modern pharmaceuticals is extraordinary. This very research is based on years and years of previous research, experiments, and studies. It is a system that draws from the canon of modern science. Much of this science is based on previous science and so on and so forth. Is the system perfect? Definitely not, but if I were to give you any advice about pharmaceutical drugs, it would be this. What works for some, does not always work for everyone. When and if you find a drug that works for you, which expresses little to no side effects, then it has the ability to change your life for the better and heal you in a very profound way.

My experience with anti-depressants was not always a positive one. I started out, like many other people, being adamantly against anti-depressants. Every time my doctor would suggest them, I would reject her offers. I truly believed that they would stunt me in some way and would damage my brain. It was this irrational belief that was holding me back from getting the aid I needed to get better. It didn't help that the first drug that I did try did not

264

work very well. It was a drug that also doubled as a smoking cessation drug. It did not help my depression in any way. It, in fact, made me feel worse. After I had stopped taking it, I was convinced that anti-depressants didn't work. When my major depression hit, and my doctor friend came to visit me, he suggested another type of antidepressant known as a SSRI, which stands for Selective Serotonin Reuptake Inhibitor (SSRI). These classes of drugs are generally more effective in dealing with depression. What he told me was that I needed to find the right match in order to have success. At that time, I was in such bad shape that I agreed to try one. I was desperate. My friend, being a doctor of internal medicine and infectious diseases, would often prescribe SSRI antidepressants to AIDS patients who were terminally ill and subsequently depressed. After about three weeks of taking that particular drug, it made me feel about 10% better. Now, at the time I still did not feel that great at all, so it didn't feel like that much of an improvement, but the drug did help me to start to climb out of the terrible state that I was in. After a few weeks, it put me in a place where I could gain some control over my life again. That in itself was worth the risk in taking it. That's the point of these types of drugs. Not to necessarily completely heal you, but to get you out of a damaging state and into one where you can have some semblance of control in your life again. I was on that particular drug for about a year and decided that I did not want to take it anymore and stopped. There was still a part of me that didn't want to be on drugs. For whatever reason, I was still under the impression that drugs were harmful. After about six months of being off of it, I got hit hard with something that I had rarely experienced before, anxiety. I was at my brother's wedding in the Caribbean, and I experienced a debilitating anxiety where I began to dry-heave every morning again. I even began to throw up on a daily basis as a result. This was reminiscent of my walks with my friend when I first got diagnosed with major depression. When I got back home, I immediately went to my family doctor, and he put me on a low dose of yet another SSRI antidepressant. Now, this particular drug worked much better than the last SSRI I had been on previously. After about two weeks, my anxiety symptoms disappeared, and I felt like myself again – in fact, I felt strong. This time it felt like I had finally found the right drug for me. The right fit. This drug worked very well with my chemistry. It did not express any side effects in me, and I started to feel better only after a short time of taking it. It was then that I realized that the right drug can change your life for the better! But I was so convinced that drugs were bad. It was very enlightening and humbling.

For me, taking anti-depressants is something that I may have to do for the rest of my life. I have made peace with that fact. What I had to learn very quickly was to become comfortable with the shame associated in our society with taking drugs for mental illness. I needed to get rid of my own shame about it as well. Our society drills into us, at a very early age, that if you can't handle things on your own or cope without the aid of drugs, then you are lesser or weaker. It is a fallacy that seems to hold truer to mental illness, than to any other type of illness. One would be crazy ever to argue that a cardiac patient shouldn't take drugs because he "really should suck it up and fight it on his own." Yet, with mental illness, that is the stance that is taken by many. I had to recondition my own prejudices against antidepressants and get over my own biases. Just the mere fact that a drug helped me to regain control in my life again solidified a new idea. I began to realize that it was the same as taking a blood pressure pill if I happened to have high blood pressure. Those patients don't feel defeated for taking drugs. They do so because it helps them regulate an imbalance. And so it follows, that I needed to take an antidepressant in order to rebalance my chemistry back to normal. That is all. Once I made that distinction, all of the negative stigma and shame surrounding drugs started to melt away. I realized that all of that shame was within my own head. It was my ego's way of telling me that I was too weak to fight it on my own. I learned that this type of thinking is poisonous: it was keeping me from reaching my best life. My doctor told me something very interesting. He said that I may have to take an antidepressant for the rest of my life if I wanted to be able to feel okay. At first, that angered me. I didn't want to be dependent on anything for that period of time, but the more books I read and the more research I did, I learned that the right anti-depressant can make your brain function normally again. Once I saw the positive results and started to do well again, I started feeling like living proof that drugs do work and aren't evil. My suggestion to you is that whatever prejudices you may have against pharmaceuticals, try and rationally deal with them. Try out different drugs and if they don't work for you, then stop taking them. Just understand that the right drug may be out there for you, and it may be the right fit in your fight against depression.

Now, you may at times feel like a lab rat trying all the different anti-depressants, and the worst part of it is that you are doing it when you feel terrible already. But if you are diligent and careful, you may be able to find one that works for you. That can have a profound effect on the rate at which you get better. Drugs are not a cure-all by any means. They are, though, a way of giving yourself a chance to get a leg up on the disease. I still take my little white pill every morning and am now in a place where I am at peace with it. I know now that it is a vital component in my battle against depression.

Step 9 - Sleep

"A good laugh and a long sleep are the two best cures

for anything."

-Irish Proverb

It is my true belief that sleep is one of the most

important, if not the most important, component

of healing. Nothing has more of a rejuvenating

effect on the body and the brain as sleep. It is very important to cultivate healthy sleep patterns – what psychiatrists and doctors often term as, Sleep Hygiene. The problem is that people with depression either sleep too much or sleep too little. They are often out of sync with their natural rhythms when it comes to sleep. In this regard, I would say that if you are getting too much sleep, it is definitely better than not getting enough. When I was in the midst of the worst part of my depression, I would only sleep around 4 hours a night. I would wake up early in the morning and not be able to get back to sleep. These early morning wake-ups had a negative effect on my mental state, in that I never felt fully rested and was more prone to frustration and anger than I had ever been. My nights were restless, and it often took a long time for me to actually get to sleep. I often felt hopeless as I stared at my ceiling, thinking of all that had gone wrong with my life. What I learned then was that my mind was a beast and that I needed to do everything in my power to tame it. If left alone, the mind can rant and rave into the night and work you up to the point where you cannot rest. Those sleepless nights were filled with anxiety and despair, but they prompted me to seek a way of quieting my mind so that I could finally drift off to sleep. One thing that I learned very quickly about sleep was that it is, in many ways, about routines. When I did the same thing every night in my preparation for sleep, it helped me to get ready for it and settled my mind to start winding down. What I did in my pre-sleep preparation, slowed down my mind so that I could fall asleep. I started to take a warm shower every night before bed and prayed right before I went to sleep. The prayer had a relaxing effect on my mind, and it helped me to stop thinking of myself and release my troubles and anxieties to a Higher power. Once I was done, I would get into bed and lay on my back and try to empty my mind of all thought. I would try to focus on my breath. The more thoughts that came to my mind, the more I would just let them go like they were powder dissolving into a vast ocean of consciousness. Sound familiar? One by one, the thoughts would show up, and I would watch them dissolve and then my mind would clear into emptiness again for a brief moment. Then, back to my breath. Eventually, those brief moments turned into periods where my mind was empty and peaceful. As those moments grew, I could slowly start to feel my eyes roll to the back of my head, and I could feel myself falling into a sleep-full trance. Thoughts would appear less and less, and eventually, there would be a blackness followed by the appearance of vivid pictures. Those pictures were dreams. I would be asleep. This was not easy at first, and it took some time to practice but it was based on the same principles as my meditation practice. The fewer thoughts I had, the better. The more I practiced emptying my mind, the easier it got for those pictures to show up.

Sleep is a very elusive thing for those who are stressed because they are often stressed about not being able to fall asleep! The longer it takes to fall asleep, the more stress they have about it. The routine of the warm shower, the prayer, and the meditation helped me to create my own ritual of sleep. Now when I go to bed, it does not take me very long to drift away. You must create your own ritual in order to find your path to sleep. You must learn to slow things down in the evenings, as you get closer to bedtime. Try to find relaxing rituals that will work for you. Turn off the phone and laptop at least two hours before bed. Try a warm cup of chamomile tea and some soothing music instead. Meditation and yoga also help before sleep. Try different soothing rituals and see what works best for you.

Let's talk a little about melatonin. Melatonin is a hormone that regulates sleep and wakefulness cycles. This hormone is crucial to your body's ability to regulate its sleep patterns. When you suffer from insomnia, these patterns are not functioning properly. Getting good sleep is all about balancing your circadian rhythm. In a study that was published in The Journal of Neuroendocrinology, C. Cajochen, K. Kra uchi and A. Wirz-Justice conclude that melatonin can be beneficial for insomnia by inducing phase shifts and advances in human circadian rhythms. In their research, they conclude that melatonin supplementation is not only good for sleep, but it also has positive effects during the waking hours because the body's circadian rhythms are restored to normal.

If you are having trouble falling asleep, it goes without saying, that you may want to stay away from caffeinated drinks after 5 pm. Heavy exercise in the evenings is also not the best idea. What I found worked best for me, as I mentioned before, was to stick to my pre-sleep routines as well as drink kefir before bed. Kefir will raise the melatonin in your system naturally and flood your body with stress-reducing B vitamins that will calm you before bed. This I found, is much better than taking a melatonin supplement as they are often hit or miss when it comes to effectively raising your melatonin. The problem with supplements is that they are not always as bioavailable as the natural sources. They cannot, therefore, be as easily absorbed into your system. Kefir is all-natural, and your body absorbs and uses the melatonin in it very easily. Just remember to get the effervescent kefir – it has a lot more beneficial bacteria than the non-effervescent kind. About 25 ml before bedtime may help you fall asleep about 15 minutes after drinking it. It has always worked for me. The natural melatonin in the kefir will also start to regulate and balance out your natural circadian rhythms and get them back on track. If you are still having troubles with your sleep, you can also always seek out a reputable sleep clinic. Sleep clinics are great for pinpointing what you need to do for your particular situation. Also remember, you can see your doctor and have her prescribe a sleeping pill if need be. Sleep is incredibly important, and if you are not getting enough, it can be disastrous. As we went over before, there is no shame in using pharmaceuticals to get things back on track.

Step 10- Fasting

"Fasting of the body is food for the soul."

-Saint John Chrysostom

When I was in my mid-twenties, I fasted a few times, and it taught me a great lesson. The lesson was that what you put into your body will affect you in profound ways. Here's how I learned it.

After a day of fasting, I decided to break my fast with a big greasy fast food burger and fries. Immediately afterward, my body went into shock: I felt so sluggish and sleepy that half an hour later, I was in a veritable self-induced coma. I was useless. Well, the next time I fasted, I decided to break my fast with freshly squeezed orange juice, a moderate portion of rice, chicken, and a big salad. As a result, I had expansive energy and felt great. I was bouncing around all night and ended up going out with friends. This lesson on how fatty and fried foods affected me was never forgotten. Even though I knew that I shouldn't eat those types of foods, I continued to eat them for another 5-6 years until my major depression hit. I did eventually learn that it is imperative that I break my fast with healthy foods in order to replenish my body the right way and feel good thereafter. What fasting did was intensify the effects that the good or bad food had on me. Just by not eating anything during the day, I was able to see what effect certain foods had on my mood and energy.

Now, we've already gone over what foods will make you feel better, but here I want to talk about the practice of fasting. Fasting has many benefits, and we will go over a few of them now.

Fasting is an effective way to detox your body. When you fast on a regular basis, your body naturally leeches out many of the toxins within it and cleanses itself as a result. Fasting also helps you get stronger and improves both physical and mental performance. In a study conducted on intermittent fasting, one group of scientists concluded the following:

Several cross-sectional and longitudinal studies have shown that intermittent fasting has crucial effects on physical and intellectual performance by affecting various aspects of bodily physiology and biochemistry that could be important for athletic success (Cherif).

In fact, more and more studies show that intermittent fasting is good for human health. In terms of the brain, in her TED talk titled, You Can Grow New Brain Cells. Here's How, scientist, Sandrine Thuret, describes what actions are beneficial for neurogenesis or the promulgation and creation of new brain cells. She mentions intermittent fasting as among the few things you can do in order to create more new brain cells every day. She also mentions omega-3s, antidepressants, exercise, turmeric, fruits rich in color (like blueberries) and sleep, all of which we have talked about already.

The other great thing about fasting is that during the fast, your body goes into a shock-state. As a result, your body naturally produces more testosterone and growth hormone. This production, in turn, helps you to feel great, stay young, and also ensures that you recover from exercise more rapidly. In fact, there is a study published in The Journal of Clinical Investigation that is titled, Fasting enhances growth hormone secretion and amplifies the complex rhythms of growth hormone secretion in man. This particular study found that intermittent fasting can increase growth hormone by a very large amount, naturally (Ho et al.) For both men and women, increases in testosterone and growth hormone are good things. Both of these hormones help the body you heal after workouts as well as produce a natural drive in order to accomplish your daily goals. Fasting is, in my opinion, the real fountain of youth. One that will enable you to look and feel younger, as well as give you the strength necessary not only to fight off your depression but to thrive thereafter. The best part of it is, that your body does it completely naturally.

The health benefits of fasting are very powerful, but in my experience, I find that what it does in order to fortify your ability to control yourself is just as important. Once you have fasted a few times, you will realize that you have more self-control over your urges and impulses than before. What fasting does so well is that it helps you to build and strengthen the muscle of restraint and self-control that is necessary for success. I found that the more I fasted, the easier it was for me to forge my will-power into steel. I started to gain control over my own negative bad habits. It really allowed me to take my time before making decisions about my health. I felt that as a result, I began to have full dominion over my choices. Over time, I became much less impulsive. Being spontaneous is great when it leads to fun and healthy things, but when it leads to toxic, destructive behaviors or bad diet habits, it is much better to have control. The solidification of my self-control is probably the most single, powerful and beneficial side effect of consistent fasting.

Once intermittent fasting is a habit in your arsenal against depression, you will find that your ability to control your cravings for unhealthy foods is strengthened. You will also find that when you fast, you will actually crave certain foods. These foods are often the foods that your body needs. The body is highly intelligent in that it will often crave what it is missing. Fasting magnifies this autonomic trait. Just be careful, if you are craving foods that are high in fat, sugar, carbs, or are processed, or fried, use your new found willpower to avoid them.

For me, fasting also has a spiritual side. I personally found that the spiritual benefits of fasting were incredibly soothing to my mind, body, and soul. I always felt grateful after a day of fasting, in that I realized how lucky I was to have food and water when I broke my fast. I felt closer to my Creator, and it calmed me and made me feel at peace with the world. This practice also prompted me to think about the poor, the needy, and the hungry. I began to help others when I got a chance. I found myself volunteering at the homeless shelter three times a month as well as donating to help feed the homeless. It had to do with the fact that I now knew what it felt like to be hungry. I knew what it felt like to be in their shoes. I endeavored to help others as a result of that realization. A friend of mine once told me that helping others is the most selfish thing you can do because it makes you feel so good. I have to say that he was right. A large component of my healing in regard to depression was to help others heal. It was what helped me to take the focus away from myself and focus on others. In a way, that gave me a break from the constant analysis of how I was feeling all the time. This became the eventual impetus and motivation behind writing this book. Perspective is everything, and when you help others who need it, you begin to notice the positive changes in yourself that allow you to be strong enough to do so. This is how you leap from being a victim of your own illness, to begin to be able to use your knowledge to help others in their struggle. This is also how you may ultimately be able to give your illness a meaning that is beyond the story of your life – one that branches out, to the stories of others.

Try fasting. Choose the method of fasting that is best for you, and don't be afraid. It is not as hard as you fear it to be. The parameters that I use are super simple. I just refrain from food and water in the daylight hours. As soon as the sun sets, I break my fast. You can do it too. Once you've done it a few times, you will discover that it is much easier than you expected. After a few successful fasts, you may find that a funny thing may happen: you may actually look forward to it. I currently fast every Thursday, and I look forward to it every week as a way to cleanse my body, strengthen my mind, and calm my spirit. It is also a wonderful way to connect with my Creator. That in itself is worth the effort.

Step 11 – Mindfulness

Practice

"Breathing in, I calm body and mind.

Breathing out, I smile.

Dwelling in the present moment I know this is the

only moment."

-Thich Nhat Hanh

As we progress, we begin now to see what exactly the little things are that I mentioned at the beginning of this book. In my particular battle with depression, it was all about the combination of exercise, supplements, diet, breathing, and sleep. When I managed those things well, I began to change the physiology of my body and brain, and it helped to slowly heal my depression. If my brain was a computer, you could say that the hardware was being repaired as a result of all these actions. With time and effort, I started to feel better. As I felt better, I took on more at work and soon found myself in a managerial role. With that, I needed to become not only better at handling my own life but, in a way, begin to help others with theirs as well. What I learned is that I needed to be stronger and not prone to any kind of relapse if I was going to succeed in a leadership role. What helped me to find this steadiness and strength was mindfulness practice.

As time passed, I did not waiver from my routines and stayed-the-course regarding those all-important little things. But, I was still missing something. That something was the ability to handle my mind and my thinking in an effective way. My mind was still wild and out of control, and I needed to tame it and direct it. Mindfulness practice was the new software that my computer needed. I had to get rid of the bugs. In my research and experience, I discovered that my depression had a duality. One part had to do with how my brain physiologically functioned, and the other had to do with my thoughts and thought-processes. Negative thought-patterns often had just as powerful an effect on my moods as physiological impairments such as mental fog and low energy. I found that when I had thoughts that bothered me, or I was overly self-critical, I would feel discomfort and I would want to withdraw from others. I often found myself ruminating for days on-end on memories or thoughts that were painful. This would manifest as a negative self-image or as terrible memories of past failures and would make me feel consistently awful. I would run through, over and over, the traumatic events of my past, and it was hard to shut off my brain. At the time, I felt like I had no control over what I thought about. I was at the mercy of these constant negative thoughts, and it was affecting the quality of my life in a dramatic way. I felt like I had no way of stopping it and would endlessly repeat the pattern over and over. I would often talk about the same fears and distresses to my friends, all of the time. At the time, my friends were my only pillars of support, and I felt like even they were getting tired of hearing me agonize about my insecurities. I did find that by incorporating physical exercise into my daily routine, I was able to find some relief from the thoughts for brief moments, but often the next day, I would again find myself in those same dark corridors. It was as if every morning I would wake to negative thoughts, and it would take me the rest of the day just to try to fight myself out of it. What I eventually discovered

306

was, that in order to quell those negative recurring thoughts and make sure that I could regain some semblance of control again, I would have to take a more active role in consciously fighting them off. But, it is not easy to fight off negative thoughts. They can be persistent and, in many ways, we tend to believe everything we think on a regular basis. What gives our thoughts power over our moods are our beliefs. The belief in the validity of our negative thoughts drives us to feel awful about ourselves. But how does one get out of that mindset? How do you let go? How I got out of that mindset was the mindfulness practice that I'm about to share with you. Before we get into that, I must say it started with the realization that my mind was out of control and I was able to recognize that my thoughts were working against me. I realized that in order to fight off the negative thoughts and the fear that was prevalent in my life, I needed to adopt an incredibly important and powerful idea: Don't believe everything you think. When you are in a state of depression, you must realize that everything you see and evaluate is filtered through a dark lens. How you see the world and others are, often, a negative version of reality. Further to that, how you see yourself when you are in this state is much more critical and damaging than when you are in a healthy place. People in a state of depression are very good at picking themselves apart. What you must learn is that you have to be good to yourself. Just like you wouldn't kick a loved one when they are down, you must learn not to kick yourself when you are down. One method is to learn to talk-back to that voice that constantly criticizes you or looks at things in a negative manner. This can be very effective, but like anything else, it takes practice. You must learn to recognize when your thinking is off and observe it. Simply notice it. See it. Then, you must learn to jump in and defend yourself when your thoughts go in that direction. One great way of starting all of this awareness is the practice of mindfulness.

Mindfulness is nothing more than the awareness of your inner-self and how you are reacting to the world around you. The more you are aware and observing your thoughts, the more you will have control over them and be able to guide them to a better place. In many ways, as I mentioned before, your mind needs to be tamed, and you can tame it by controlling its focus. One thing that you must understand is, whatever you focus on every day, is what your life will ultimately be. If you are always focusing on your weaknesses and your failures, then you will no doubt feel impotent and weak most of the time. The problem is that when we are in a constant state of rumination about our failures and shortcomings, it is hard to get out of it consciously. We are stuck. We can't just think our way out of it. It is so real and prevalent that we get sucked into the drama of it and cannot think of anything else. The way to break the pattern is to consciously and mindfully focus your attention on something else. And that something else is nothing other than your breath. If you have already started the meditation practice that is outlined at the start of this book, you will certainly be able to practice wakeful mindfulness as well. When I was overwhelmed by my thoughts, to the point of insanity, I began to voraciously read books on mindfulness. Each one outlined a different way for me to use mindfulness to break out of my negative thought patterns. The great news was that they all had very similar ideas. They were all centered on the simple act of redirecting your attention. This was primary to all of them. How each book outlined this practice was also very similar. They all broke things down into steps and made it into a practice that was easy for me to take on. These books were instrumental in allowing me to battle my negative thoughts and to quell my thoughts of fear and anxiety. As a result of the research that I have done on the subject, I eventually came up with my own version of a mindfulness technique. This practice works very well for me, and I hope that you may be able to use it as well. I call it, SAFE 7. I found that this was the best and most efficient way for me to use mindfulness, to direct my mind to a better place, when I was in a state of rumination or had negative thoughts. As I practiced SAFE 7, I learned that mindfulness was a very simple and effective remedy for directing my mind. I just had to keep practicing it. SAFE 7 works. The reason is its simplicity. I utilize it anytime I get a negative, fearful, or disturbing thought. I just go through the steps – one at a time. The simple steps of the SAFE 7 method are as follows:

SAFE 7 Mindfulness Method

1. S stands for SEE IT: When you have a negative thought, painful memory, or find your mind going in a bad direction, the first step is to see it. Just see it and notice

it. Pretend you are floating above and you are watching yourself react to this negative thought. Also, notice the thought without judgment. Just see it and notice how it's making you feel.

2. A stands for ACCEPT: The second step is to accept the thought. Accept everything about it. Do not condemn it or reject it. Just accept. Be okay with the thought or memory and let it be. Try and look at it from a distance and accept it. That is all.

3. F stands for FOCUS: The third step is to

let go of the thought and focus on your breath for 7 long and deep seconds. For a moment, let it go. Try not to think of anything at all. Focus on your breathing and feel your stomach move in and out in a diaphragmatic breath. Do this for 7 long and deep seconds. When any thoughts come into your mind, just re-focus on your breath. This may be hard to do if you're feeling very emotional about the thought but just be in the present moment and focus on your breath. If it helps, try and see the numbers appear in your mind, one by one. Do not attribute anything to the numbers, just see them appear as you count to 7 and slowly focus on your breath.

4. E stands for Engage: After your breathing is done, take a moment and engage with the present moment. Look around and see that the world is bright as a result of coming out of that momentary deep focus. Engage with the world around you. Engage with the thoughts and ideas that make life good. Engage with what you can do right now to make things better. It could be to take action, it could be to be

easier on yourself, and it could be to simply let yourself rest. Engage with what is important in your life and what matters. Engage with what is meaningful in your life. Engage, and come to the present moment.

Once you have gone through these four steps, you will find that the initial thought that bothered you has less power over you. If you are still very bothered by it, do SAFE 7 again. See it. And once again accept it. Don't try to get rid of it. Just accept it. Then, focus on your breath for seven long and deep seconds. After that, re-engage with the world and the present moment. Just remember to do each step one at a time with patience, and with your full attention. Practice this method over and over until you get good at it. The more you practice this, the better you will get at it, and the more you will be able to direct your mind to where you want it to go, not where it wants to go. By practicing this method every time you have a negative thought you are strengthening and redirecting your mind. It is like a workout for the focus of your mind. What you are doing is taming the beast by directing your attention down to your breath when it's wild and out of control. What you are teaching it is that you are in control. Keep directing your mind back down to your breath, and you will be training it. If you do this enough times, then you will gain control where your mind goes. The more you practice this exercise in mindfulness, the more you flex the muscle of thought-control in your mind. Soon, you will find that you will always be attuning your focus to your breath when you are uncomfortable – directing your thoughts so that you have full control of your inner state. When you do this on a consistent basis, you will find that the world around you will consequently become more vivid and burn brighter. This will happen every time you re-engage with the present after your breathing. What this practice ultimately does is propel you into the now.   You will find that you will naturally and effortlessly re-engage with the world as a result.

Mindfulness practice has been proven to help with both depression and anxiety. It has been shown to increase the size of the brain and has also been shown to balance-out brain functions. In his book Mindsight, Dr. Daniel J. Siegel outlines how, if we practice controlling our focus and directing our attention, we can not only improve the firing of our synapses in a positive way but can also change the physical structure of our brains for the better (795). This is a very powerful finding.

Mindfulness will help you break out of your recurring negative thoughts and forge a new path of control regarding your mind. What often goes hand in hand with mindfulness is the ability to stay in the present moment. When you practice the SAFE 7 method regularly and take the time to focus on your breath, you will notice that you will feel yourself leaving either the past thought that was bothering you or the future anxiety that is tormenting you and come back to the present very easily. I often find that as I take my attention down to my breath, I feel my mind silencing and resting as well. When I come back to the world around me, I find that I am more aware of my actions. My actions actually start becoming an exercise in meditation thereafter. I also find that the thought that was tormenting me so badly ceases to have any more power over me. I often practice SAFE 7, as I am driving, or doing dishes, or even looking at the horizon. If I'm having stressful thoughts or discomfort, I focus my attention on my breath. As I breathe, I feel the world around quiet down. Then as I come out of the breathing, I re-engage and see the world anew. At that point, I know I have been brought back to the present, and at that point, I think of how to re-engage. I think of what I can do to improve the situation and how it can help me to grow. For me, SAFE 7 has been very powerful when I practice it throughout the day. It has helped me to soothe the anxieties that pop-up. In this regard, it has been a life changer that has helped me with thoughts and emotions that are not very productive. Mindfulness practice has always taken me to a place that is not only healthier but has helped me to find a pathway to peace in my life.

Now that we have talked about mindfulness practice, I want to talk about the incredibly high prevalence of fear in depression. You must understand that fear and anxiety are incredibly common in people who are suffering from depression. When we are depressed, we are more susceptible to irrational fears about our life, our present, and our future. This fear can be debilitating, paralyzing, and overwhelming. It can take over our consciousness, and we could spend hours upon hours going over the same thoughts over and over. In a way, we become trapped in its cage. These thoughts of fear can seem larger than life and incredibly real. They can be quite vivid and work us into a frenzy of anxiety. At times, the cage gets smaller and smaller, and we feel that there is no way to win or no solution. What you need to understand is that the majority of that fear is your imagination, creating stories that just aren't true. What is happening in actuality is that your mind is preparing you for the absolute worst. By preparing you, it creates a myriad of worst-case scenarios and challenges you to find solutions to these horrific possibilities. This is a mechanism that humans have acquired over millions of years of survival in order to prepare for the worst. When we are depressed, this mechanism is out of sync and working on over-drive. It is therefore incredibly heightened during bouts of depression and when we are stressed and anxious. These fears can feel very real and paralyze us. Even though these attacks of anxiety and fear can be relentless, mindfulness practice can help. The better you get at SAFE 7, the better you will be able to direct your mind when it is under attack – just start practicing it. I know that when you are in a constant state of fear, it can be really hard to think your way out of it. So don't. Just begin to direct your mind and your thoughts to your breath – over and over. Keep at it, and you will find a drug-free way of directing your mind to a healthier place. Just

understand that it is not a one-shot thing. You

will need to practice SAFE 7 every time you get

attacked by negative thoughts or are consumed

by irrational fears. It can help you to win the

fight.

Step 12 – Gratitude

Practice

"Wear gratitude like a cloak and it will feed every

corner of your life."

-Rumi

Over months and months, as I became more

mindful, I began to direct my mind to things that lifted me up and made me feel good, instead of dwelling on my shortcomings or the painful mistakes of the past. At that time, I began to feel that I had not only come a long way in terms of my depression but had come a long way as a human being. I had struggled and fought through bad days as they came up and pushed myself to engage with the world and those around me. I learned that every day was a battle and also an opportunity to learn something new. I knew that I needed to continuously try to persevere but also had to keep exploring. As I had more days where I felt good again, I began to realize that I needed to take more of an active role in maintaining the good feelings I was having. The only way to do this, I learned, was to begin to appreciate the positive things in my life on a consistent basis. At that time, the past was still very painful to think about. It was hard for me to make peace with the illness that had caused me so much grief and the memory of so many dark nights still lingered. That's when I came across a program that helped me to heal emotionally. I began to listen daily to an audio recording called Daily Magic. It was part of the Get The Edge program by Anthony Robbins. This Daily Magic recording guided me through a series of exercises, which included deep breathing, gratitude, visualization, and positive incantations. Out of all the parts of the Daily Magic program, the gratitude portion affected me the most. In fact, in many of the books that I read on the subject of happiness, gratitude practice always came up over and over. At the beginning of this book, I mentioned how you could beat your depression and eventually thrive. Well for me, as soon as I started a gratitude practice, I began to learn how to thrive. I found that, just by the simple act of focusing on the things and people in my life that I was grateful for every day, I was able to enjoy my life in a new and surprising way. I started to feel happier, and I felt at peace with everything. Peace with my depression, peace with my relationships, peace by appreciating everything. As I began to practice gratitude every day, it reminded me of what I had, and I experienced the sudden realization that I was indeed, a rich man. The Anthony Robbins gratitude practice guided me through the process of focusing on the people, places, and things in my life that brought me happiness. It helped me to notice and fully experience all of the qualities of this world that I love. Not only what I owned, but who I loved, and who loved me. I began to germinate and grow the idea of being grateful for everything that gave me joy. This practice started to improve my relationships and made me realize that I already had everything that I needed – both within myself and all around me. Even though I did not have a wealth of material things, I had a wealth of the necessary things in order to feel happy. Things like, good food, a place to live, great friends, and a great family. I had access to great music, great art, great films, great literature, and bounds of information that made my life better. Taking the time to focus on these things made me feel amazing! I practiced it every day, and it always took me out of my low moods and propelled me into a state of contentment. I realized that gratitude was a very important ingredient in my daily happiness. The fact is that all of the research on this subject completely supports what I found out. In almost all of the literature that I read on the subject of happiness, I found, that the majority of them reference cultivating a habit of gratitude. Some mention that a gratitude practice can actually change the nature and structure of your brain and can rewire you to feel happier. In one study researchers found that subjects who used mindfulness or gratitude practices diminished their stress and depression and increased their happiness levels. They found that when the subjects took happiness tests like the Edinburgh Depression Scale, the Perceived Stress Scale, and the Subjective Happiness Scale, they scored better than those who did not perform mindfulness practice or gratitude practice. They also found that those who stuck to it had a better sense of overall well-being (Leary and Dockray). These practices are not only effective in making people happier, but they have also been known to change the physiological structure and elasticity of the brain! They are very powerful if done regularly.

So, how do you get good at being thankful and feel great as a result? In this next section, we will go over how you can easily start your own gratitude practice. Before we get to the mechanics of it, though, I must stress that like the other suggestions in this book, gratitude practice must be practiced! It's probably the one step in this book that will be the most overlooked because people tend to think that it is not really necessary. The truth is that it is hard to set time aside and mindfully map out everything that we are grateful for. My suggestion to you is that you take a few minutes every morning and focus on the things that make you happy. As a result, you will begin to notice that it changes how you see the world. Like almost everything in this book thus far, the habit of gratitude must be forged with discipline. It takes a commitment to consciously focus your mind, once a day, on the people, places, emotions, feelings, ideas, and technologies that you are grateful for in this world. Anything and everything that makes you happy and that you can possibly be grateful for. Now, if you are still in a bad part of your depression, this may be very hard to do because you don't feel very well or you may not be up to it. If this is the case, then it is even more of a reason to do it. If nothing else, you will be taking a few minutes to focus on the things that you appreciate. You may at times need to push yourself to go through with it, but I promise, taking the time to focus on these things will enrich your life.

Choose a time. It can be in the morning like I said before, or it can be after you meditate, or after you perform one of your mindfulness exercises, or even after you do some physical exercise. When you begin to focus on gratitude regularly, you will notice that your mind will be ready to accept it and will be ready to concentrate on something positive. All you have to do is set aside about 5 minutes. In those 5 minutes, close your eyes and flood your mind with the people, places, and things that make you smile.

Below is a step-by-step method on how you can start a gratitude practice now. This following gratitude practice is broken up into four easy steps. I would suggest that you read the captions below into a voice message and listen to it every day. You can also transcribe the captions below onto a piece of paper and read it to yourself every day (if that works better for you). I guarantee that just reading it will take you to a good place.

Daily Gratitude Practice

1. Begin to think of all of the people in your life that make you happy. Think of them one by one. Think of how they have affected your life in a positive way. Think of why you are happy that they exist. Think of how your life is richer and has more meaning with them in it. Think of

the people who make you smile just by thinking about them. They can be people you know closely or people who you have just met. Think deeply about these people. These are the people that make life worth living. How are they special? How do they make you feel about yourself? How do they make you a better person? Why are they so good? How do they make you better? Are they funny? Are they caring? Are they kind? These are the people that you love. These are the people that love you. Think of these people one by one. List them and list their qualities. Think of how special they are and why they make your life great. Do this for about one minute until you are smiling.

2. Begin to think of all of the places in your life that make you happy. These are the places that you are grateful for and that make you happy just by remembering them. Think about why you like these places. Are they beautiful? Are they calming? Are they exciting? What makes these places so great? It can be a room in your house, or a spot in your backyard, or

a tropical paradise. Think of them as vividly and colorfully as you can. Picture them as being real in your mind, so that you can visit them anytime you want. Begin to think of how you feel when you are relaxing in these places and how lucky you have been to be able to go to these places. Think of the joy that they have brought to your life. These are the magical places in this beautiful world that either make you feel safe and comfortable or bring you wonder and awe. Think of why you are grateful that these places exist. Do this for one minute until you are smiling.

3. Now, think of the things that make you happy. Think of these special items and the story behind them. How are they designed? What do they look like? What are these things? Why do they make you so happy? Do they serve a function that gives you pleasure? Are they fun? Are they cool just to have? Why are you so grateful for having these things? How lucky are you to have these things that enrich your life? Think deeply about these things for about one minute until you are

smiling.

4. Begin to think of all of the information in this world that makes you happy. The music, the movies, the books, the technologies, the games, the pictures, the shows, the activities – everything that you look forward to seeing or doing that gives you pleasure. Think of how lucky you are to have access to all this information. Think of how it makes you laugh. Think of how, at times, they may move you to tears. Think about how you have learned from this information. Think of how this

information makes your life better. Think of what you will discover next and how it will help you to get smarter. Think of how this information will make your life richer and make you feel better each day. Think about these for one minute until you are smiling.

5. As you focus on all this, think of all of the reasons why your life is good and begin to look for all of the good things that will show up in the days ahead, These good things will make you smile, give you peace, and give you joy. Think about the

endless possibilities that await you. Think of what you can discover. Think of what you can experience. Think of all the ways you will succeed. The things you will create. The way you will grow. The people you will help. Think about all of the reasons your life is good for one minute until you are smiling.

This daily practice changed my life for the better. After I had practiced it each day, I began noticing all of the good things in life. I began noticing all of the little things that I appreciated about this world. With this awareness, I found that more good things began to show up in my life. As I began to appreciate the people in my life that I loved, they ended up becoming closer to me – as if by magic. As I loved certain books or movies or technologies – they became more meaningful. As I thought of the wonderful places, I was able to retreat to them anytime I wanted. We tend to take for granted, the little things around us that make our lives rich. When we start noticing them again, then we start being grateful for them again. As our awareness of them grows, it makes them all come to life again. It is another form of mindfulness, to appreciate everything as it comes into our realm. Your life becomes richer just by noticing the good in it and appreciating the good. If you stick to it every day, it can help you see life in a whole new way.

Step 13- Light Therapy

"A single sunbeam is enough to drive away many

shadows."

-St. Francis of Assisi

If you are lucky enough to live in a sunny climate year-round, then this step may not apply to you. For the rest of us, especially those of us in northern climates, light therapy is something that is definitely a must in the late fall and throughout the winter. For many sufferers of depression, Seasonal Affective Disorder (SAD) is a real thing. It can be characterized as a low mood during the fall and winter months due to the lack of exposure to sunlight.

For me, I always notice the effects of Seasonal Affective Disorder sometime around late November. Like I've mentioned before, I began to learn how to keep my depression at bay by using everything that we have talked about until now. I continued to do all of the little things and executed them on a daily basis. These days, I manage to keep my depression in remission for most of the time, but I still notice a drop in my energy and mood sometime around late fall or early winter of every year. I am never myself during this time of year. This past year, in particular, SAD hit me really hard. Around early December, I was feeling very low and was not sure why I was feeling down and anxious. Luckily, I have experienced SAD enough times at the exact same time of year to know that it has something to do with the amount of direct sunlight I have been exposed to. For this reason, from the months of November through to

February, I make sure to take walks outside and get exposure to direct sunlight for at least 20 minutes a day. No matter what the weather, I go outside. I'm lucky, in that I live next to a large open hill and I can walk up the sunny side every morning and get my 20 minutes of direct sunlight. If I can't make it, though, I make sure to turn on a full spectrum light, or SAD lamp, and sit in front of it for a minimum of 30 minutes in the mornings. The great thing about light therapy is that you feel it immediately. As soon as you turn the light on, you can sense some relief. Full spectrum lamps light up a dark room in an instant and are a good solution to the problem of not getting enough light in the winter. The important thing to remember is that exposure to these lights has been proven to alleviate the symptoms of SAD. The Journal of Depression Research and Treatment, support these facts by saying that full-spectrum lights, which are "similar in composition to sunlight" help with SAD (Melrose).

Full spectrum lamps can be an important part of your arsenal against depression, and you can get good ones for under a hundred dollars online. Just make sure that they are full spectrum lights and can be used to treat Seasonal Affective

Disorder. If you are thinking of supplementing with light therapy, be extra careful if you have been diagnosed with bipolar disorder. In some instances, light therapy may have a chance of triggering a manic episode in people who have been diagnosed with bipolar disorder. Make sure to consult your doctor before you use one.

SAD lamps have never triggered any type of mania in me, even though I was diagnosed with an affective disorder. During those late fall and winter months, it did its job. I have to admit that for me, it was always about remembering to turn the light on in the mornings, as I would often forget. I also sometimes don't start using a SAD lamp, until it is a bit too late and the lack of light has already started affecting my mood in a negative way. I find, though, as soon as I do, it starts making me feel normal again after only a few days of use.

These lights have been shown to have an effect on your natural circadian rhythms. You will find that they may balance out your sleep cycle as long as you do not use them too late in the afternoon or at all in the evenings. My suggestion is to treat these lights as a preventative measure against depression during the late fall and early winter. I always use them

from early November all the way to the end of

February.

Step 14 - Quitting

smoking

"Never ever, ever, ever, ever give up."

-Sir Winston Churchill

In the midst of the best and the worst parts of

my depression, I was a very heavy smoker.

Depression and smoking go hand in hand. Nicotine is a stimulant, and it often makes depressed patients feel (real or not) that it is helping them get through the worst of it. My psychiatrist even suggested that nicotine was good for me and that it was okay if I smoked during my depression. I now think back to it and realize that she was trying to illustrate a point: that depressed people tend to self-medicate with nicotine, more than any other drug, and that they do get some relief from it. I would never recommend starting to smoke in order to alleviate any depressive symptoms, though. The simple fact of the matter is that many depressed people already smoke and use smoking to cope. My suggestion in regard to smoking is that if you are already a smoker, then hold off quitting until you get to a better place in terms of your depression. Meaning, don't put too much pressure on yourself to quit when you are in a bad place. Wait until you feel a bit stronger. Throughout your depression, always try to soothe yourself, to calm yourself, and to help yourself. It is crucial that you eventually put smoking aside, but I am a proponent of handling only one crisis at a time. If you are already a smoker, and you are in the middle of the worst part of your depression, then continue to smoke.

Take your time and do everything else in this book to eventually start to get yourself to a place where you can quit. When you are stronger, and I guarantee you will eventually be stronger, you can start to begin thinking about quitting. If you are feeling better, and are in a place where you can see yourself taking the leap to quit smoking, then this next part is for you.

As a smoker, this chapter can change your life. In my struggle with nicotine addiction, I lost many battles. Over and over, what I learned is that the war is never over with smoking – whoever has the last laugh wins. Whether it's you that urges you to smoke or the little devil on your shoulder, just know that every single day that you do not smoke – you win. We've already talked about the power of breath in our daily lives, and how through diaphragmatic breathing, we can practice meditation and mindfulness in order to aid our mental and stress health. Well, it should follow then, that the power of breath can also help you to quit smoking. We'll get to that in a bit, but first, to break it down, we need to get one thing straight. In order to quit, you must want to quit very, very badly. You must reach a level where you cannot stand the idea of smoking another day, another hour, or another minute! If you have already reached this point, then your chances are good. If you have not, then you must start to cultivate a long and convincing argument as to why you need to quit right now and why you will not stand to live with smoking in your life for another minute. Write out a list of reasons and carry it with you as you smoke. Refer to it again and again and solidify your reasons for quitting. This will be the impetus for your action. Once you have a nice long list and have read it for at least a week, then you will be ready to take action. If you are going to quit, then you need to take at least three days off from work or school to do it. What you need to remember is that the first three days are the hardest. After that, it gets easier and easier. During the first three days, the withdrawal symptoms will come in close waves and depending on how heavy a smoker you are, these waves can last anywhere from 30 seconds to a couple of minutes. The key is to expect them and prepare for them when they come. These withdrawal attacks are not fun, and they can magnify any problem that you may be going through. If you get bad news or remember a bad memory, then they can exacerbate the discomfort of that thought that you are feeling. Just remember, if you are under attack from withdrawal, it does not last forever. The simple key is that every time you experience it, you must go down to your breath and breathe through it for about 20 seconds. In the first three days, you will be doing this a lot. But as the days pass, you will find that the withdrawal symptoms will be farther and farther apart from each other. As time passes, they will also be less and less aggressive in severity. As you notice this, it will become easier to breathe through the rough patches. Anytime you feel the craving coming on, just remember to breathe heavily and diaphragmatically for 20 seconds. You will not only feel better afterward; you will actually feel

366

relaxed. Breathing through these attacks will help you to win.

Before you quit, you must make sure to tell yourself that you will not change your personality in any way as a result of your quitting. That's right, your personality! What I mean by this is, that it can be easy to succumb to fits of anger and frustration when you are quitting. Don't become a jerk. Make sure to make a conscious effort to try to remain calm and cool, as much as you can, in the first two weeks. Take control of your emotions during this time. Make it a game. Tell yourself that nothing can change the nature of your cool and calm character (even if that's not entirely true). Keep breathing through it. Remember this: if you can quit smoking, you can literally do anything that you put your mind to thereafter! Use this as motivation to follow-through and not give up. Embark on a mindful decision not to lose your temper. Practice this self-control in the first week, and you will find as the weeks go on you will not only get stronger, but you will also start to feel in full control of all your emotions as you quit. The best part of quitting smoking is that you will start noticing the health benefits of not smoking right away. Your body will begin to feel better almost immediately. When you smoke regularly, it is like going through life with a large backpack full of heavy rocks on. You are always short of breath and feel tired all the time. You are also constantly reaching for a cigarette, to stimulate you for a brief instant – just to feel tired and sluggish thereafter. When you finally quit, it is like taking the backpack off. After a few days, you will start to notice that your energy levels will increase naturally and that your breath will get fuller and stronger. The simple fact is that you're not poisoning yourself every hour or two anymore. If nothing else, look forward to this. Also, anticipate the future freedom of not being addicted anymore.

Remember to hydrate with water throughout this process. Water will not only help you cleanse your system, but it will help you rid the nicotine and toxins out of your body. As you drink more water, also remember to do some aerobic exercise to aid in the cleansing. It will help with the stress. This exercise could be a run, jog, or even a brisk walk. Just make sure to move, and come to a sweat. When you do this, you will notice that you will feel stronger and begin to build on the fact that you are now a non-smoker and living a new healthy lifestyle.

Another thing to remember is that, if you feel a craving coming on, do not turn to food for help – only your breath. You will notice that you will be enjoying food more and more in the days after you quit. It is a natural reaction for your body to replace one pleasurable thing for another. Make sure to stick to the rule of eating to 3/4ths full. Don't overdo it with food or snacks or you will gain a lot of unnecessary weight when you are quitting. Just keep breathing, moving, and cleansing with water.

Also, change your patterns around. If you always go out to a certain place to smoke, then change that routine. Still, continue to go outside, but go to a different place and breathe or meditate. If you would reward yourself with a cigarette, after working long hours, then instead, reward yourself by calling someone and laugh with them instead. Treat yourself in different ways. Listen to a song that you love or take a break by watching a funny video. Switch things up. You are a non-smoker now and not tethered by the nicotine ball and chain. You are free to do whatever you want in order to feel good from now on. You will need to be creative in order to beat this. Like I said before, you will notice as soon as you quit smoking, your energy will go through the roof! Remember that oxygen is your best friend. By utilizing the oxygen that is all around you, the withdrawal symptoms will get easier and easier to deal with. Completely change your routines. Remember, this is the new, strong you that doesn't smoke and who is healthy and in control. Just know that you can feel great just by breathing.

As you reach the three-month period of not smoking, remember that even one single puff of a cigarette will take you back to square one. Try not to have a single drag of a cigarette, after you have quit. If you do, you will be starting over from scratch and will have to go through all of the pain of quitting again. Make sure not to smoke when you drink alcohol or when you have coffee. Make sure not to break, when you see an old friend who smokes and says, "Come on, lets have one together." Do not give in to it. Mentally prepare yourself for these types of situations beforehand. Visualize being offered a cigarette and saying no. Visualize having a few too many drinks and wanting one, then picture yourself saying, "Nope, I won't ruin the momentum!" I guarantee you will have the argument with yourself about whether or not you should have one. Or worst yet. You may even convince yourself to give up the whole thing and go back to smoking again. Don't give in to it. Trust me; it will not make you any feel better. If anything, you will feel defeated because you gave up. Remember your list of why you absolutely must quit. Re-read your list if need be. Carry it with you in those first three months. Stay the course. Before you know it, you are breathing your way to the six-month mark, and you are free from the prison of addiction. The freedom from nicotine is amazing, and that freedom is the best part of quitting.

I have to share with you now that I used to

smoke more than a pack a day! I was extremely addicted and very dependent. I would have a cigarette within the first minute of waking up and would constantly use nicotine, throughout the day, to treat myself, soothe myself, or just drown myself in a self-destructive way. Smoking was my way of romanticizing my struggle. At times, I felt like it was the only friend I had. But, I learned that all of that was a lie. I learned that smoking was nothing more than a destructive habit that was weighing me down in terms of my health and happiness. The worst thing about it was that the more I did it, the worse I felt physically. What I eventually discovered, was that simple breathing and mindfulness could make me feel better than any cigarette.

How I quit, was not easy. My plan of attack was to get away from the smoke. For me, it was all about changing my nicotine delivery system. I went from cigarettes to cigars, to nicotine gum, to e-cigarettes, and then finally to quitting all of it – cold turkey. In a lot of ways, cold turkey is the only way. The key is to get mad and finally have enough! You may not succeed the first time you try to quit, but just remember, every time you attempt to quit, your chances of succeeding get better. It's been proven. However impossible you may think quitting is and however many times you get bombarded by withdrawal symptoms – you can hold on. You can get through it. Just never forget: millions of others have gotten through it and you can too. You are strong enough.

Step 15 – Conquering Stress

"Life is ten percent what happens to you

and ninety percent how you respond to it."

-Lou Holtz

Everywhere you look, nowadays you see articles

and books related to the negative effects of stress. Over the years, there have been innumerable studies that prove the link between stress and disease. The dominant prescription, or suggestion from health practitioners, is to suggest to their patients that they should somehow eradicate stress from their lives. That prescription can be very nearsighted on their part. We all know how stress is a big part of life and how consuming stress can be. We also know how hard it is to get ourselves out of a stressful state when we are fully in it. It is also sometimes very difficult to get out of stressful conditions. After all, stress is all around us and could be a very big part of our day-to-day lives. If we are not careful, stress has the ability to consume us. Now, the mindfulness helps, the diaphragmatic breathing helps, and so does physical exercise, but when the stressors are constant, we often can find it very hard to escape from them. For me, my perception of stress changed as soon as I watched a particular TED talk. It changed my life at that time that I saw it and continues to change how I look at stress. The talk was by Kelly McGonigal, a health psychologist, and it is called How to Make Stress Your Friend. I deeply encourage you to see it, but I want to break down what she says in that talk right here for you. The main thesis of her talk is that the manner in which we think about stress changes the effect it has on us. Simply put, when you think of stress as energizing you and prepping you to have the courage to meet your challenges, it helps you to do exactly that. When you think of it as hurting you and making you weaker, it does exactly that as well. You see, how you view stress is how you manifest it and ultimately how stress expresses itself in your body. She explains that even the physical symptoms of stress such as sweaty palms and rapid heartbeat should be viewed by you as your body preparing itself to face challenges. When you look at them this way, stress takes on a different meaning, a more positive one and does not harm you. By simply shifting your perspective, in regard to the state you are in, you begin to take action towards making your situation better. In her talk, she mentions how your blood vessels will constrict if you view stress as harmful thereby causing potential damage to your heart, but when you view stress as helpful, your blood vessels remain open and therefore do not harm your heart. The crazy thing is that she has all of the science to back this up. To me, this is a miraculous example of how your mind can alter your physiology for the better. When you look at the uncomfortable feeling of stress and view it as your body prepping you to be courageous or helping you to be prepared, you will find that the stress will not seem as bad. It will be like reframing it in the best way possible. In fact, from my experience, I found that I became braver and more capable as a result of thinking this way. This concept of reframing stress is very powerful, in that it shows us that we can change the effect that stress has on us just by how we think about it. In a lot of ways, therefore, stress itself can help us to grow to new levels (McGonigal).

What I eventually found out about stress, on my

own, was that the difference between being stressed in order to perform highly and stressed in order to survive was very similar once I reframed all stress in the context of performing at peak levels. In his book The Talent Code, Daniel Coyle describes what it takes to reach brilliance. He talks about, how putting yourself in difficult situations, where you struggle and make mistakes, pushes you to reach higher levels of your performance. When we push ourselves to the edges of our comfort zone, when we are stressed and unsure, when we push to persevere – that is when we grow the most. That is when we reach new levels (18), although it is all dependent on not falling apart. When we are overly stressed, we are often on the edge of breaking down and losing all control. If we change our perception of that experience, we may be able to transmute it into one that gives us courage and helps us to make it through. As I mentioned before, the best news is that Kelly McGonical had all of the research and statistics to back it up. She shared that people who perceived stress as something useful actually lived longer than those who perceived stress as toxic. This concept is very much to our benefit, in that, we can use it to foster the belief that no matter how bad our stress gets, it is helpful.

Another brilliant idea that Kelly McGonigal shares in her TED talk is that stress actually makes us have closer relationships to those around us. She states that when we are stressed, we release oxytocin, the hormone related to social bonding. Oxytocin allows us to form closer bonds to those that we share our stress stories with. It also has the dual effect of protecting our heart cells and keeping our blood vessels open so that we live longer. This, on the whole, incurs much less damage to our hearts. This information is very intriguing and helpful in allowing us to change the meaning we have about stress in order to empower us to deal with

387

it in a more productive way (McGonigal).

I have personal experience with using these principles about stress in order to get myself through stressful times. As a manager, there were days my stress levels were very high, and I found that it was hard to get myself out of that stressed state throughout the day or when I came home after work. It would often follow me around, and there was nothing I could do to get unhooked from it. There was a period of time that I was dealing with a particularly stressful situation that could have resulted in my dismissal, and I was, needless to say, under an incredible amount of stress. I felt its effects on my mind and body. I was in a fog of stress, and I could not think straight. I kept creating terrible scenarios of losing my job, my house, my source of income. I kept thinking that I was doomed. I then watched that TED talk on stress. I realized then that the more I thought of it as a game and used the uneasy feeling of stress to propel me into action and courage, the more I became stronger. It took practice and the phrase "fake it 'til you make it" kept coming into my mind because there were times where I felt like I was just convincing myself of something I didn't really believe. But something special happened, the more I looked at all that stress as a vehicle to make me act and summon courage, the more I was able to actually have more courage and really live it, not just fake it. That experience was invaluable because I grew as a result of it. That stress helped me to get to the next level. When I utilized it in a useful way, it helped me to deal with my problems surprisingly well. Soon thereafter, there wasn't a problem that I couldn't deal with. It really became about understanding that stress can be your friend, as Kelly McGonigal says in her talk. She outlines that the key is (the next time you feel stress coming on) to say to yourself:

This stress is here to help me. To kick me into action. To make me realize that this is important. To help me grow into the person that can handle it. (McGonigal)

There is a phrase that I love and has helped me throughout the years, and it is: "God doesn't give you anything that you can't handle." When dealing with stress, just know that it is there to help you to act. And that if it is in your life, then you absolutely have the capacity to handle it with grace.

Step 16 – Fostering Relationships

"Love bears all things and endures all things."

-I Corinthians 13:7

There were times throughout my depression where I felt more alone than I had ever felt in my life. I knew that, ultimately, no one could get me through my illness other than myself and that no one could really understand what I was going through. At times, I resented my friends and family for not being able to relate to what I was experiencing. I often felt like no matter how much I tried to describe my depression to others, they just did not understand, or even worse; they were powerless in making me feel any better. What I learned at that time was that just the act of talking to them, engaging with them, and, however hard, connecting with them, made me feel better. I learned that the relationships in my life, however small, ultimately helped me to persevere and gave me the strength to carry on –

if not for myself, then for the love of others. For

me, my friends were my saviors as they would

often tell me the truth of what was going on and

not what I thought was going on. Like I've said

before, when you are in a state of depression

your ideas are skewed in a negative light, and

you often see things as being much worse than

they really are. Friends can help you to see

things as they really are and are able to guide

you and reveal to you that your thinking may be

off. They are also able to listen. Just listen. I've

come to learn that just the act of telling your

concerns to someone and having them listen, can

be incredibly effective in healing the emotional wounds that you experience during depression.

Family relationships are just as important. I often think that if it wasn't for the strength of my family ties, I might have been a homeless man in my thirties walking the streets, bewildered and lost. The fact that my family gave me an opportunity to rest and heal without judgment was crucial to my recovery. I spent many years living with my parents, and they never discouraged me from living at home or pressured me to go back to work too early. The fact was that because of the state that I was in, I could not work. At the time, my mother and father not only gave me the support and guidance that I needed, they gave me the space I required to heal at my own pace. This was incredibly important to my recovery. It also helped that they got involved when I began to research the solutions in regard to getting better and learned as much as I did when I was fervently seeking answers. It is important that the people around a depressed person are as educated about the disease as the person going through it and help to contribute to their fight. This concept of teamwork, when it comes to dealing with the problem, will help the depressed person to feel like they are not alone and that they have a safe and harmonious environment to get better in. After all, one of the major problems with depression is that often family and friends think that there is no problem in the first place. They simply do not believe the people who are going through it. They can often say things like, "Suck it up" or "It's just in your head," thereby exacerbating the situation and making the ill person feel like they have to prove their illness to everyone. It helps immensely if all those involved can actively get involved in the solution, instead of trying to determine if there is a problem in the first place.

Healthy relationships are therefore very important to the recovery process, and as much as one would love others to step in and help in the fight, they are not always cognizant of what to do or what steps to take. My suggestion is that you must take the first step, in reaching out to others and connecting with them, in order to build the foundations of a future support system. It is my adamant belief that "you get what you give," and by reaching out to those you love, as well as creating new relationships with those who can help, you can start to build your own support system, and that can help you win.

Here are seven actions that you can take right now to engage with others and make your relationships better.

---

7 Ways To Connect

1. Call or meet a person who is in your life right now, and let them know how much they have helped you throughout your life. Whether in good times or bad, let

them know the positive effect they have had on your life just by being alive. Let them know you appreciate them and that they make your life better.

2. Call or meet a person who you have not talked to in a long while but who you know to be someone of value. Reconnect with them, and let them know that you haven't forgotten about them. Re-engage with them, and let them know that it would be great to have them in your life again.

3. Thank a family member for being there for you (whether or not you have always had good relations with them). Let them know that no matter what occurs; they are an important part of your life and that your connection to them is unconditional. Forgive them, if you need to, and start to heal the relationship. More importantly, acknowledge that person and the value and love that they bring to your world.

4. Connect with someone in your life that you know needs your help right now. Offer to help them in any way that you

can. Reach out to them, and let them know that you will be there. Just the action of helping someone else that you love will lift you up.

5. Join a club or a group that will bring you into contact with others. They can be people who are going through what you are going through. They can be a group of people that endeavor to build or create something positive. They can be a group of people devoted to helping each other express themselves in a positive way. These groups are great for reconnecting

with your community and getting out there and meeting like-minded people. Get into the habit of talking to people about the things that you are passionate about.

6. Teach what you know to others. Find a skill that you are good at and help to teach it to someone, so that they too can become good at it. Just by virtue of passing your knowledge and wisdom to someone else, you will connect with others in a way that will enrich your life and theirs.

7. Have faith in people. Understand that just
    as you are going through your struggles,
    so is everyone else. Give people the
    benefit of the doubt. Whether it's
    strangers or people you know very
    closely. Make sure that you do your best
    to nurture every relationship. This can be
    with family, friends, workmates, or
    anyone for that matter. Get into the habit
    of trying to see the good in others. It can
    spread like wildfire.

These steps can help you to engage with others

in a positive way and help you to begin to create your own support system. You are not alone. Take the first step by reaching out to others.

I came to find that the building of healthy relationships with people was unbelievably helpful in my fight against depression. However, what I eventually learned was that the building of good relationships was not only important to do with people, it was also important in regard to nature and animals. The fostering of these types of connections always gave me relief in terms of dealing with my pain and helped me to begin to appreciate the world and all that it

406

contains.

Leonardo da Vinci said, "The wisest and noblest teacher is nature itself." When I first began retreating into nature, I found that it was an immediate relief to my relentless thoughts and uneasiness. Those environments and habitats always made me feel just a little bit better by virtue of me being in them. They also gave me an added opportunity to observe the beauty that surrounded me as well as engage fully, with all of my senses again. From the smell of the trees and flowers to the feel of an ocean breeze on my face, to the sight of the ever-changing skies, the natural environment always had a way of soothing me by ensconcing me in its natural, positive energy. I've never needed piles of written research to tell me that exposure to thick forests, grassy hills, long beaches, and blue lakes would naturally alleviate some of the stress that I was under. In fact, when I began taking daily walks to the hills around my house, I began to realize that my connection with nature was a very important part of my life. I learned that it was an essential and necessary component in my experience as a human being. This relationship with nature became, for me, the cornerstone of how I could have time to myself while at the same time being completely connected to the natural world. When I would walk through the woods, I would incorporate diaphragmatic breathing in order to relax and cleanse and also use mindfulness techniques in order to be fully present in the experience. These excursions into nature became sacred moments that would help me to begin to find slivers of joy in the midst of my darkness. As my illness got better, those same walks in nature became moments of true bliss. The key was that as I developed the habit of going into nature when I was feeling low, it became an instant remedy for feeling better. I eventually started enjoying it more and more, and now as a result I try to be around nature at least once a day. I often multitask and execute my daily workouts in a natural landscape. Exercising in natural environments can be incredibly synergistic, and it's a hell of a lot of fun.

Along with the engagement to nature, the positive effect that animals can have on the human psyche cannot be overstated. Animals have a natural ability of sensing and soothing our pain in a way that people do not. I remember that there were days when, as a family, we would retreat to my uncle's acreage for the weekend, and I would come into contact with the horses that were on the property. Just seeing and being in the presence of those magnificent and majestic animals, calmed me and gave me relief.

Any domestic animal that you like, and come into contact with, can make you feel loved and happy just by being in its presence. For those who want to adopt an animal in their life, they find that the animal can help them to take care of and love something, even though it may be hard for them to take care of and love themselves. This notion automatically takes a person out of themselves and their problems and helps them to focus on how to take care of an animal. For example, the fact that they have to get up and go outside to walk the dog can help to build good habits when it comes to moving their way into feeling good again. The affection and physical interaction with animals can also make them feel immediately better if they're having a rough day. Interactions with animals do not have to be limited to owning one – a lot of people visit friend's animals and even go to the zoo or the pet store for a quick dose of love and relief when they need it. Incorporating a routine that involves animals is definitely a great way to have a positive interaction that can make you feel better immediately. Studies have even found that simply seeing pictures or videos of baby animals releases stress and makes us happy. That is the powerful and profound effect that the world of animals has on human happiness.

These connections to other people, nature, and animals are what helped me to start seeing the beauty of this world again even when there were times where I felt like there was nothing I could enjoy. They were tiny steps towards life and were, in my case, tiny steps towards love. If you are in the worst part of your depression, these things can, at times, seem pointless, but I urge you to continue to take these steps towards others, nature, and animals. They may ultimately be the things that can help you to see the good in life again. Who knows, the people that you interact with may just need your help in the future. How great would it be if you could return the favor?

Step 17 – Building

Resilience

"Man never made any material as resilient as the

human spirit."

-Bernard Williams

I want to be able to tell you that you can

completely eradicate depression from your life forever, but if I did, I would be lying to you. The truth is that your battle against depression will be fought throughout your life. It will be ongoing. What you need to know and be prepared for is that it may raise its ugly head in times of stress and during times of major life changes and challenges. The good news is that if you do the little things we have talked about in this book, you can be prepared for it when it comes around. In my experience, because of the changes that I have made in regard to my lifestyle when bad things happen to me, I can now deal with them much better than before.

These events could be things like losing a job, a death in the family, or a traumatic experience. When these types of things happen, I do still feel the effects of depression, but they are natural, and I am able to deal with them until they pass by naturally and in their due course. What I ended up realizing is that these types of events, however bad, are not as catastrophic as being in the middle of a major depression. Having said that, we all need to know that relapses can happen and it can be because of the fact that we are not following through on the healthy choices that we know we should be making. We reach for unhealthy food or stop exercising when we have a bad day. When we make bad choices, it can activate those depression genes in our bodies. I urge you not to fall into the trap. Be disciplined. There will be times when you will be tested, and you will, for sure, have down days. Those are the days where you will really need to follow through and stick to the game plan. On those days, you won't want to do anything. On those days, I encourage you to always push-through and act. Go through with the exercise, the meditation, the mindfulness, the breathing, and so on. When you are having a bad depression day, or you are getting attacked by negative thoughts, I want you to remember to

418

do the following:

What to do when you are under Attack

- Dive head first into something productive such as work, hobbies, chores, or anything that requires your focus and concentration. I know it's hard to concentrate when you are in a depressed state, but if you focus on a specific task, you will be surprised at how quickly you can transcend your state and move on to something productive and even creative.

- The key is to remember that nothing lasts forever. If you are down, then it is a temporary state that will pass. For the time being, get busy and work on something. Before you know it, you have resolved something, or even better, you have created something new.

- Be careful not to make any rash decisions. In this state of mind, limit big decisions that involve your life. Wait until a better time to address these. Wait until the storm has passed, and look at those types of decisions when you are in a more optimistic frame of mind.

- Watch your diet! As you try and get through this, remember that your diet is the key. The better and cleaner you eat, the better you will feel. Good food is everything. Freshly squeezed juices, fruits, vegetables, and probiotic foods will help to decrease the severity and duration of your depressed states.

- Remember to stay the course in terms of exercise. If you start skipping days because you don't feel up to it, then you may get worse. Even fifteen minutes of cardio will give you some relief. Just make sure you come to a sweat. Even if you don't feel better immediately after exercise, the benefits will compound. Make it into an unbreakable habit. You will definitely feel calmer after a workout, and it can help you feel more relaxed as well as surprisingly energized at the same time.

- Meditate or pray. A simple meditation regiment will ease the distress you are in. As with anything, it must be a practice that you develop. The more you do it, the better you will get at it. Try and do it twice a day for a minimum of at least 5 minutes each session.

- Connect with friends. Talking with friends for even a few minutes will help. Try and think of a funny story to tell them and even ask yourself, "What is funny about this?' Try and help them with their problems, and this will make you forget yours – it works like magic!

- Don't believe everything you think! During this period, your thoughts can and will go sideways. Everything from your self-image to how you think others perceive you. Don't believe everything you tell yourself because chances are you are seeing things through rose-colored glasses. Try to see things as they are – the best way to do that is to see them as better than they are.

- Don't feel discouraged. Just because you

have a few bad days or a bad week or a

bad month, does not mean that you can't

fight off depression. Life is often cyclical.

You will be able to fight it off again and

again throughout your life. You now have

the tools, and you will be able to use them

whenever you need them.

Final Thoughts

"I am not what happened to me,

I am what I choose to become."

-Carl Gustav Jung

Throughout the last few years, my ability to fight off the waves of depression has been my biggest challenge. The truth is, every time depression comes around again, I always think, "Is this going to be as bad as before?" "Am I going to be able to fight my way out of this again?" Even though I am in a much better place to be able to handle it, I always have a tiny little thought that it might come back in full force. This, I have learned, is completely natural and is a by-product of the traumatic experience that I have lived through. What I discover over and over again is that when it does come back, and I turn to all those little things that helped me before, I am able to feel good again relatively quickly. In each previous instance, I would fall back on what I knew to be true and what I knew would work. I would fall back on what helped me to win the battle. I eventually learned that the disciplined actions that had gotten me this far will help me get out of any new predicaments that I find myself in the future. It all comes down to sticking to the original game plan. And that plan entails the 17 steps that we have gone over in this book. There are of course still days where I still feel down, or I feel overwhelmed, but I'm able to hold on much better now and overcome those feelings a lot quicker than before. I remember reading somewhere that the difference between happy people, and those who are not, is that happy people don't dwell as long on their failures and bounce back within a couple of hours. Whereas, those who are unhappy tend to ruminate on their failures for days after they happen. Don't get stuck in negative thoughts. Take your attention down to your breath and then re-engage with the world in a new way. Every moment is a new opportunity to start-fresh and build on something good. Focus on the things that can help you to find peace and happiness, adventure and fun – whatever your mind desires and whatever you want to create. You will find that as you heal, your ability to create your world the way you want it will improve. Your ability to enjoy life will improve. Your ability to move on will improve.

As we end our journey, I want you to be able to start looking for and finding a meaning behind your pain. The meaning that this depression ultimately had for me was that it became a spiritual warning-sign. That warning sign was a reminder not to take for granted all of those periods of health that I enjoyed throughout my life before. My depression reminds me to enjoy life and live it to its fullest when I am healthy. I must say that I now absorb and savor every single atom of life and delight in every tiny part of it – the good and the bad. I have learned now, to look forward to each new day and each new surprise that comes along. When I look back on the struggle, the future always revealed itself to me in good ways as long as I hung on long enough to give it a chance to do so. I want you to remember that there is a reason why you needed to go through this and that reason is yours alone. Find it, and let it help you to overcome as well.

I want you to refer to this book again and again throughout your life so that you can ensure that you have the tools you need to gain control and enjoy your life to its fullest. Be patient. These steps do not take effect overnight. You must slowly make them a part of your existence. A part of who you are. Keep at it, and don't beat yourself up if you are not doing every single step perfectly. As I've said throughout this book, see what works for you and slowly add another step. True healing takes work, but if you have some self-control, you will get there. Remember to take your time and be patient. Whatever you do – don't give up.

In closing, I have to share with you one more thing. In those first few years of my struggle with depression, there were many dark nights where I felt that I could not go on any longer, and the idea of ending my life was so prevalent that it consumed every part of me. I have to tell you that I am incredibly grateful that I did not succumb to, or act on, any of those thoughts or feelings. I learned to start fighting harder. I knew I had to, in order to survive. I realized that those dark nights were necessary so that I could finally start making some real changes in my life. Those changes led me to eventually experience my life in a whole new way. I must share with you that after I got through the storm, and started to do things in a drastically different way, I felt like my life was resurrected. I felt like a newer, better version of myself. I always think of the metaphor of the raging forest fire and its devastating effects – of the enormous destruction and the barren aftermath; but also of its propensity to create a new, stronger, greener, forest thereafter. A re-genesis of sorts. This is the renewal and rebirth that we all go through when we are stricken with any disease. Yet, if we survive a consuming and catastrophic illness, the aftermath is that we enjoy life much more than before. In many ways, this illness was a warning that my body gave to me in order to tell me that I must change my lifestyle and begin to do things in a different way. In many ways, it was like that fire, in that, it burned away all of the toxic habits that were holding me back and keeping me from becoming a stronger version of who I needed to become. That fire is cleansing. It can be very scary and upsetting, but believe me, if you have started your own journey – you are on your way to a better place. My ultimate hope is that one day you will be able to thrive and make your dreams come true. I also know that you will be very proud of the way that you were able to handle all of it. Just keep in mind, you never know what you can discover in the days ahead or what bliss may be around the corner, just waiting for you.

The Beginning (not The End)

You made it! Thanks for reading. If you enjoyed this book and it was helpful in any way, please take a moment and review it on Amazon. If you have, then I greatly appreciate it. Your review will help get this book to many sufferers of depression, who can use it to get better. Also, please feel free to visit my website Dreamlevelnow.com and visit the Dream Blog for more helpful information on, health, wellness, and living your best life.

With love, Nima.

Works Cited

"10 Proven Benefits of Green Tea." *Authority Nutrition*. N.p., 2016. Web. 30 Dec. 2016.

Aune, Dagfinn, Nana Keum, Edward Giovannucci, Lars T. Fadnes, Paolo Boffetta, Darren C. Greenwood, Serena Tonstad, Lars J. Vatten, Elio Riboli, and Teresa Norat. "Whole grain consumption and risk of cardiovascular disease, cancer, and all cause and cause specific mortality: systematic review and dose-response meta-analysis of prospective studies." *Bmj* (2016): I2716. Web.

"BBC Radio 1 - BBC Advice - Depression." *BBC News*. BBC, n.d. Web. 02 Jan. 2017.

Bellino, Silvio, Paola Bozzatello, Elena Brignolo, Chiara Brunetti, and Filippo Bogetto. "Omega-3 Fatty Acids Supplementation in Psychiatric Disorders: A Systematic Review." *Current Psychopharmacology* 1.4 (2012): 353-64. Web.

Breymeyer, Kara L., Johanna W. Lampe, Bonnie A. Mcgregor, and Marian L. Neuhouser. "Subjective Mood and Energy Levels of Healthy Weight and Overweight/obese Healthy Adults on High-and Low-

glycemic Load Experimental Diets."
Appetite 107 (2016): 253-59. Web.

Cajochen, C., K. Kräuchi, and A. Wirz-Justice.
"Role of Melatonin in the Regulation of
Human Circadian Rhythms and Sleep."
Journal of Neuroendocrinology 15.4
(2003): 432-37. Web.

Chainani-Wu, Nita. "Safety and Anti-
Inflammatory Activity of Curcumin: A
Component of Tumeric (Curcuma
longa)." *The Journal of Alternative and
Complementary Medicine* 9.1 (2003):
161-68. Web.

Cherif, Anissa, Bart Roelands, Romain
Meeusen, and Karim Chamari. "Effects of
Intermittent Fasting, Caloric Restriction,

and Ramadan Intermittent Fasting on Cognitive Performance at Rest and During Exercise in Adults." *Sports Medicine* 46.1 (2015): 35-47. Web.

"CHLORELLA: Uses, Side Effects, Interactions and Warnings - WebMD." *WebMD*. WebMD, n.d. Web. 30 Dec. 2016.

Cohen, J. F. W., M. T. Gorski, S. A. Gruber, L. B. F. Kurdziel, and E. B. Rimm. "The Effect of Healthy Dietary Consumption on Executive Cognitive Functioning in Children and Adolescents: A Systematic Review." *British Journal of Nutrition* 116.06 (2016): 989-1000. Web.

Conklin, Sarah M., Peter J. Gianaros, Sarah M. Brown, Jeffrey K. Yao, Ahmad R. Hariri,

Stephen B. Manuck, and Matthew F. Muldoon. "Long-chain Omega-3 Fatty Acid Intake Is Associated Positively with Corticolimbic Gray Matter Volume in Healthy Adults." *Neuroscience Letters* 421.3 (2007): 209-12. Web.

Coyle, Daniel. *The Talent Code: Greatness Isn't Born: It's Grown, Here's How.* New York: Bantam, 2009. Print.

Devassy, J. G., S. Leng, M. Gabbs, M. Monirujjaman, and H. M. Aukema. "Omega-3 Polyunsaturated Fatty Acids and Oxylipins in Neuroinflammation and Management of Alzheimer Disease." *Advances in Nutrition: An International Review Journal* 7.5 (2016): 905-16. Web.

Erejuwa, Omotayo O. "Effect of Honey in Diabetes Mellitus: Matters Arising." *Journal of Diabetes & Metabolic Disorders* 13.1 (2014): 23. Web.

Ford, Patricia A., Karen Jaceldo-Siegl, Jerry W. Lee, and Serena Tonstad. "Trans Fatty Acid Intake Is Related to Emotional Affect in the Adventist Health Study-2." *Nutrition Research* 36.6 (2016): 509-17. Web.

Fujii, Kiyomu, Yi Luo, Rina Fujiwara-Tani, Shingo Kishi, Song He, Shuyun Yang, Takamitsu Sasaki, Hitoshi Ohmori, and Hiroki Kuniyasu. "Pro-metastatic intracellular signaling of the elaidic trans fatty acid." *International Journal of Oncology* (2016):

n. pag. Web.

Gadiraju, Taraka, Yash Patel, J. Gaziano, and Luc Djoussé. "Fried Food Consumption and Cardiovascular Health: A Review of Current Evidence." *Nutrients* 7.10 (2015): 8424-430. Web.

Gopinath, Bamini, Victoria M. Flood, Annette Kifley, Jimmy C. Y. Louie, and Paul Mitchell. "Association Between Carbohydrate Nutrition and Successful Aging Over 10 Years." *The Journals of Gerontology Series A: Biological Sciences and Medical Sciences* 71.10 (2016): 1335-340. Web.

Ho, K. Y., J. D. Veldhuis, M. L. Johnson, R. Furlanetto, W. S. Evans, K. G. Alberti, and M. O. Thorner. "Fasting Enhances Growth Hormone Secretion and Amplifies the Complex Rhythms of Growth Hormone Secretion in Man." *Journal of Clinical Investigation* 81.4 (1988): 968-75. Web.

Kelly, John R., Paul J. Kennedy, John F. Cryan, Timothy G. Dinan, Gerard Clarke, and Niall P. Hyland. "Breaking down the Barriers: The Gut Microbiome, Intestinal Permeability and Stress-related Psychiatric Disorders." *Frontiers in Cellular Neuroscience* 9 (2015): n. pag. Web.

Kim, Sang-Hyun, Hyun Seok, and Dong Suk Kim. "Relationship Between Serum

Vitamin D Levels and Symptoms of Depression in Stroke Patients." *Annals of Rehabilitation Medicine* 40.1 (2016): 120. Web.

Leary, Karen O', and Samantha Dockray. "The Effects of Two Novel Gratitude and Mindfulness Interventions on Well-Being." *The Journal of Alternative and Complementary Medicine* 21.4 (2015): 243-45. Web.

Lorenzo, Arianna Di, Seyed Fazel Nabavi, Antoni Sureda, Akbar Hajizadeh Moghaddam, Sedigheh Khanjani, Patrizia Arcidiaco, Seyed Mohammad Nabavi, and Maria Daglia. "Antidepressive-like Effects and Antioxidant Activity of Green Tea and

GABA Green Tea in a Mouse Model of Post-stroke Depression." *Molecular Nutrition & Food Research* 60.3 (2015): 566-79. Web.

Martínez-González, Miguel A., and Almudena Sánchez-Villegas. "Food Patterns and the Prevention of Depression." *Proceedings of the Nutrition Society* 75.02 (2016): 139-46. Web.

Masley, Steven. "Dr. Steven Masley: PBS Special." *30 Days to a Younger Heart with Dr. Steven Masley*. PBS. N.d. Television.

Mcgonigal, Kelly. "How to Make Stress Your Friend." TED Talks.

Melrose, Sherri. "Seasonal Affective Disorder: An

Overview of Assessment and Treatment Approaches." *Depression Research and Treatment* 2015 (2015): 1-6. Web.

Moore, Thomas. *Dark nights of the soul: a guide to finding your way through life's ordeals.* New York: Gotham , 2004. Print.

Nabavi, Seyed Mohammad, Maria Daglia, Nady Braidy, and Seyed Fazel Nabavi. "Natural Products, Micronutrients, and Nutraceuticals for the Treatment of Depression: A Short Review." *Nutritional Neuroscience* (2015): 1-15. Web.

"Nordic Seminar on Glycemic Index: From Research to Nutrition Recommendations." *TemaNord Glycemic Index* (2005): 83-84. Web.

Pedersen, B. K., and B. Saltin. "Exercise as Medicine - Evidence for Prescribing Exercise as Therapy in 26 Different Chronic Diseases." *Scandinavian Journal of Medicine & Science in Sports* 25 (2015): 1-72. Web.

Perlmutter, David, and Kristin Loberg. *Brain Maker: The Power of Gut Microbes to Heal and Protect Your Brain--for Life*. New York: Little, Brown, 2015. Print.

"Possible Interactions With: Green Tea." *University of Maryland Medical Center*. N.p., n.d. Web. 02 Dec. 2016.

R, Kim. "Observing the Effects of Mindfulness-Based Meditation on Anxiety and Depression in Chronic Pain Patients."

Abnormal and Behavioural Psychology 02.01 (2016): n. pag. Web.

Robbins, Anthony, Gerald G. Jampolsky, and Robert G. Allen. *Anthony Robbins: Get The Edge.* Robbins Research International, 1990. CD.

"Safety and Anti-inflammatory Activity of Curcumin: A Component of Tumeric (Curcuma Longa)." *Journal of Alternative and Complementary Medicine (New York, N.Y.).* U.S. National Library of Medicine, n.d. Web. 02 Dec. 2016.

Samraj, Annie N., Oliver M. T. Pearce, Heinz Läubli, Alyssa N. Crittenden, Anne K. Bergfeld, Kalyan Banda, Christopher J. Gregg, Andrea E. Bingman, Patrick

Secrest, Sandra L. Diaz, Nissi M. Varki, and Ajit Varki. "A Red Meat-derived Glycan Promotes Inflammation and Cancer Progression." *Proceedings of the National Academy of Sciences* 112.2 (2014): 542-47. Web.

Schulte, Erica M., Nicole M. Avena, and Ashley N. Gearhardt. "Which Foods May Be Addictive? The Roles of Processing, Fat Content, and Glycemic Load." *Plos One* 10.2 (2015): n. pag. Web.

Shell, Ellen Ruppel. "Artificial Sweeteners May Change Our Gut Bacteria in Dangerous Ways." *Scientific American*. N.p., 2015. Web. 30 Dec. 2016.

Siegel, Daniel J. *Mindsight: The New Science of*

Personal Transformation. New York: Bantam, 2010. Print.

Soni, S., LN Joshi, and A. Datta. "Effect of Controlled Deep Breathing on Psychomotor and Higher Mental Functions in Normal Individuals." *Effect of Controlled Deep Breathing on Psychomotor and Higher Mental Functions in Normal Individuals.* 59.1 (2015): 41-47. Web.

"The Effects of Two Novel Gratitude and Mindfulness Interventions on Well-being." *Journal of Alternative and Complementary Medicine (New York, N.Y.).* U.S. National Library of Medicine, n.d. Web. 02 Dec. 2016.

"The Scientist's Mind." N.p., n.d. Web. 2 Dec. 2016.

Thuret, Sandrine. "You Can Grow New Brain Cells. Here's How." TED Talks.

Tousoulis, Dimitris, Aris Plastiras, Gerasimos Siasos, Evangelos Oikonomou, Aleksis Verveniotis, Eleni Kokkou, Konstantinos Maniatis, Nikolaos Gouliopoulos, Antigoni Miliou, Thodoris Paraskevopoulos, and Christodoulos Stefanadis. "Omega-3 PUFAs Improved Endothelial Function and Arterial Stiffness with a Parallel Antiinflammatory Effect in Adults with Metabolic Syndrome." *Atherosclerosis* 232.1 (2014): 10-16. Web.

Welland, Diane. "Does Vitamin D Improve Brain

Function?" *Scientific American.* N.p., 2009. Web. 02 Dec. 2016.

"Why a Sugar High Leads to a Brain Low." *Psychology Today.* N.p., n.d. Web. 30 Dec. 2016.

Zhang, Yu-Jie, Ren-You Gan, Sha Li, Yue Zhou, An-Na Li, Dong-Ping Xu, and Hua-Bin Li. "Antioxidant Phytochemicals for the Prevention and Treatment of Chronic Diseases." *Molecules* 20.12 (2015): 21138-1156. Web.